Light from the Dreaming Spires

Light from the Dreaming Spires

Reflections on Ministry to Generation Y

KENNETH J. BARNES

RESOURCE *Publications* · Eugene, Oregon

LIGHT FROM THE DREAMING SPIRES
Reflections on Ministry to Generation Y

Resource Publications
An Imprint of Wipf and Stock Publishers
199 W. 8th Ave., Suite 3
Eugene, OR 97401

www.wipfandstock.com

PAPERBACK ISBN: 978-1-5326-0550-5
HARDCOVER ISBN: 978-1-5326-0552-9
EBOOK ISBN: 978-1-5326-0551-2

Manufactured in the U.S.A.   09/08/17

To Joe Martin

Contents

Introduction

In the peaceful Oxfordshire countryside a few miles from the city where I had the privilege of teaching theology and serving as a chaplain to graduate students, you will find the quaint little village of Towersey. Once famed for hosting an annual folk festival, the place consists of a pub, a manor house, a village hall, and a charming Saxon church called St. Catherine's. As with many communities of this size in England, village life has always centered on the church and Towersey is no exception. However, while people are happy to attend weddings, funerals, harvest festivals and the like, they rarely attend Sunday services and like most people nowadays, seem generally disinterested in religion. So it was quite brave of the new wardens to suggest a series of mid-week public lectures entitled 'The Big Questions'. As I drove into the village for the inaugural talk on arguments for the existence of God, my wife asked me how many people I expected to be in attendance. I was only half joking when I quipped that we'd be lucky if we had enough for a hand of bridge. To my utter amazement and delight however, we walked into a standing-room only auditorium and by the end of the evening it was clear that despite their apparent indifference to religion, these people had deep spiritual needs and thirsted for more information about God.

I suppose I shouldn't have been shocked at all. In my role as a university chaplain I saw many people who professed to be either atheists or agnostics show more than a passing interest in religion. In fact, I used to host a Saturday morning discussion group with the university's secular society, where we read and discussed the merits of Kierkegaard and C.S. Lewis. When one of the leading members of the group announced that he was considering further academic studies in theology, I assumed it was merely a matter of intellectual curiosity, but now I'm not so sure. Now I think he genuinely believed that there was something to all of this God business and he wanted to see for himself whether the extraordinary claims of Christianity, could in fact, be true.

These experiences of mine in Oxford are not dissimilar to what I encountered recently, while on a lecture tour in America. After presenting a paper at Yale University, I found myself surrounded by some deeply committed Christians, including leading academics and senior business people who desperately wanted to find ways to effectively communicate the Gospel to the next generation of academic, church and business leaders; but felt ill-equipped to do so. Similarly, after speaking at a conference in New York City, I encountered both church leaders and lay people who wanted to reach the same group of people, with very similar messages; but they too lamented a lack of practical resources applicable to their mission. That's when I decided to write this book.

That said, this book isn't intended to be a "how to" book *per se*. Far be it from me to tell anyone how to do ministry! It is however, a reflection on both my time as a university chaplain and my research into ministry to Generation Y. In it, I pay particular attention to such phenomena as: the influence of postmodernism on the beliefs, attitudes and assumptions of Generation Y; the influence of so-called New Atheism (particularly as articulated by Professor Richard Dawkins); biblical skepticism and arguments against the existence of God (as espoused by Professor Bart Ehrman); the importance of good theology and well-honed Christian apologetic skills; and most importantly, the need to establish meaningful, personal relationships (i.e. mentoring) with those whom we seek to reach with the Gospel of Jesus Christ. In addition to my personal reflections and research into these areas, I will share some stories that I hope will demonstrate some of the issues people of that generation struggle with and how I tried to minister to them in those circumstances. In order to protect people's privacy, I have constructed composites of actual events; so while none of the people I describe are real, all of the stories are true.

I hope this book will prove to be a useful resource for anyone who wants to bring the Gospel of Jesus Christ to Generation Y, including pastors, chaplains, lay leaders, academics, and everyday Christians. There are a lot of people out there, who don't currently come to church, but that doesn't mean we can't bring the church to them.

1

University Chaplaincy–An Introduction

BACKGROUND

In order to fully appreciate and understand the complexity of Christian Ministry among students at Oxford University, it would be helpful to consider the relationship between the University and the officially established Church of England (C of E). Until the University Test Act of 1871, entry into Cambridge, Durham, and Oxford Universities was restricted to members of the Church of England; no 'dissenters' were allowed. Consequently, any evangelical activity needed to come from either outside the University or from those within the University who had such leanings.

It is also important to understand the collegiate system, whereby each college enjoys a considerable degree of autonomy over the affairs of their students and the culture of their quadrangles (campuses). Alumni and other deceased benefactors heavily endow every college of the University; in fact, after the Crown, and the Church of England, Oxford University is the nation's largest landowner. Consequently, appointments to various positions of influence (including college chaplaincies) tend to remain in the hands of a select group of well-connected individuals and families. These individuals and families (sometimes derided as 'the great and the good') tend to be socially conservative, theologically liberal and very mainstream, especially in their practice of religion and are usually resistant to anything that might be described as evangelical.

In 1893, the then principal of Wycliffe Hall, Dr. F.J. Chavasse (later Bishop of Liverpool and founder of St. Peter's College, Oxford) in cooperation with the Oxford Evangelical Trust formed a new ministry designed specifically to reach the student population that became known as the Oxford Evangelical Pastorate. The Pastorate, as its charter states was designed to encourage students to embrace a 'true and lively faith' founded upon biblical principles. Remarkably, as with the revival movements of the 1730s and 1830s this movement began with a handful of faithful students (and their chaplain) meeting on a weekly basis to read the Bible in Greek. As with the other movements before them, this led not only to a period of intellectual and spiritual renewal, but a time of significant missionary activity and works of Christian charity, including the establishment of a medical mission to the slums of South London.

Over the ensuing years the influence of the Pastorate grew, but the effects of the Great War were devastating, not only to the Pastorate, but to the University, the Church, and to the nation as a whole. The wholesale slaughter of millions of men in what seemed to be a pointless struggle cast a long dark shadow over the mood of the nation. Those who had survived the war returned to university as older, battle-hardened, and cynical men whose faith had been all but shattered. Both the University and the Pastorate had to virtually reinvent themselves in an effort to effectively meet the intellectual and the spiritual needs of a very different student population. It was a difficult task, but the Pastorate, in association with the local churches did their best to bring a message of Christian hope and love to the student body and soon the Pastorate's influence was growing once more. Unfortunately, the outbreak of the Second World War wreaked havoc once again and the post-war years proved to be a very difficult time for the evangelical movement and for the English church in general.

After the War, the greatest challenge to the evangelicals was no longer an intramural debate over the nature of churchmanship or differing points of doctrine; the new challenge was to stem the tides of secularism, materialism, and indifference to all things metaphysical. The popular belief was that humanity's best hope lay with the advancement of science and the creation of material wealth and all expressions of religious faith were deemed to be nothing more than quaint reminders of a bygone era. Antireligious fervor was especially intense within the academy and in many ways the Pastorate retreated to the safer confines of a local parish, a process that had begun some twenty-five years earlier.

Over the ensuing years however, many things began to change both at Oxford University and within the Church of England. The slow decline of the established church provided evangelicals within the C of E with an opportunity to increase their influence. Recent Archbishops of Canterbury, George Carey and Justin Welby are from the church's evangelical wing and there are many evangelicals in positions of influence across the denomination. Additionally, the recent financial mismanagement of the Church's endowments has meant that local congregations have had to start paying their own way and as a rule, evangelical congregations tend to be financially (as well as spiritually) healthy. Lastly, the failure of science and unbridled capitalism to fulfill their utopian promises has prompted the current generation of young adults (Generation Y) to reconsider the truth claims of Christianity as evidenced by the phenomenal popularity of such programs as Alpha© and Christianity Explained©.

Additionally, at Oxford University there has been a tremendous shift in the demographics of the student population. Until very recently, nearly the entire student body was comprised of homegrown undergraduates, primarily from privileged backgrounds. Today however, approximately forty percent (40%) of the students are graduate students, and most of them are from outside the United Kingdom (including approximately fifteen-hundred American scholars).

This change of environment has resulted in the recent establishment of three distinct, yet closely knit graduate student ministries, with which I had personal involvement.

The first is called the Oxford Graduate Christian Union (GCU), a student-led fellowship of Christian graduates, whose stated aim is to 'encourage and challenge each other in (their) journeys of faith'. They meet regularly to explore the intersection of faith and praxis, especially as it relates to their areas of academic study. I was a member of the GCU's Council of Advisors, comprised of academics, recent graduates and clergy.

The second is the newly reconstituted Oxford Evangelical Pastorate, an extension of the original Pastorate, but no longer associated with a particular parish and re-focused on the needs of the University's graduate community.

Lastly, there was a ministry that I started myself, called the Oxford American Mission whose focus was primarily (although by no means exclusively) on the spiritual needs of American expatriate scholars (as well as their families and friends).

RELIGION AND THE ACADEMY

While anti-religious (and specifically anti-Christian) sentiment among high-profile academics is not new, recent events have created an environment that is particularly hostile towards people of faith within the academy. They include:

1. The events of September 11, 2001. Atheists have seized upon these tragic events (and the military campaigns that have followed) as an opportunity to reignite the age-old mantra that religion is the cause of most human conflict and suffering.

2. The emergence of a new strain of atheism that *Wired Magazine* (November 2006) recently called: 'New Atheism'. This new strain of atheism is no longer content with professing that God is a myth, it professes instead that the very idea

of God is malicious and should be eradicated from popular consciousness. The most ardent and prolific proponent of this New Atheism is none other than Oxford's own Professor Richard Dawkins, author of numerous tomes on the subject, including the widely read *The God Delusion*.

3. The work of biblical scholar Professor Bart D. Ehrman (UNC Chapel Hill). Professor Ehrman's books not only attack the authority and efficacy of Scripture, but the very existence of God as well. While not an atheist, *per se* (he is a self-described agnostic) his work entitled *God's Problem* is a particularly vociferous and injurious re-casting of the so-called problem of evil argument.

4. The entrenchment of postmodernity and postmodern thinking among young adults (particularly Generation Y).

QUESTIONS TO CONSIDER

These phenomena raise serious questions about how the church may effectively minister to young people in the current environment, including:

1. What are the spiritual needs of young adults (Generation Y / Millenials) and how are those needs influenced by postmodern culture, New Atheism and biblical skepticism?

2. What should a ministry to people of Generation Y look like?

3. What should be the theoretical, theological and practical underpinnings of a ministry to Generation Y?

4. How should Christians respond to the arguments put forth by the likes of Dawkins, Ehrman and others?

5. What can university chaplains and other people whose primary focus of ministry is to members of Generation Y learn from my experience as a chaplain; what did or didn't work; what may or may not be improved; and how can the various models employed be adapted to other settings?

2

Ministry to Generation Y

As Sören Kierkegaard rightly noted:

> A Church triumphant is nothing but a sham. In this
> world we can speak only of a militant Church. The
> Church militant is related to and feels itself drawn to
> Christ in humble obedience. The Church triumphant,
> however, has taken the Church of Christ in vain.[1]

In the wake of September 11, 2001 it is unfortunate that use
of the word 'militant' has become unacceptable in many Christian
circles. It should go without saying however, that Kierkegaard is
speaking metaphorically about spiritual warfare and not literal,
carnal warfare. That said, I think his point is very well taken and
useful in consideration of our current context.

The Church in the West, especially in those countries such as
the United Kingdom where Christianity is the established religion
of the state, or the United States, Canada, and Australia where
Christianity has been the dominant religion since their inceptions,
may well be guilty of taking the Church's privileged position for
granted. In doing so it has lost sight of the fact that the Kingdom of

---

1. Charles E. Moore (ed.), *Provocations: spiritual writings of Kierkegaard*
(Farmington: Plough Publishing, 2007), p. 226.

God is indeed at war with the World (James 4:4), including those seemingly benign forces that oppose the Gospel, not by confronting it head-on (although that is an increasingly popular tactic), but by undermining its power through the slow and unrelenting marginalization of its cultural influence. In her recent book entitled, *Making Sense of Generation Y* (2006) Sara Savage concludes that nowhere is this phenomenon more evident than in the prevailing attitude of indifference toward religion and Christianity that many young people currently exhibit.

In order to understand young peoples' attitudes toward Christianity and religion in general, special attention should be given to postmodernism and New Atheism in particular. In this chapter, we'll consider several approaches currently in use by the Church to address these issues and explore ways in which the Church may exploit certain elements of them (i.e. a Trojan Horse approach) as well as strategies to counter their effects head-on.

UNDERSTANDING GENERATION Y

What do we really mean by the term 'Generation Y'? Most sociologists agree that Generation Y is the generation born since 1982. They are the children of the post-war Baby-boom (my own) generation (born between 1946-1963). As Savage notes:

> Boomers are usually characterized by the counter-culture of the 1960s . . . liberal, idealistic and optimistic . . . the first young people to have access to the contraceptive pill, and (for the middle class at least) to benefit from the expansion of higher education.[2]

I can say from my own bitter experience that it was a generation steeped in ideologies as diverse as socialism and unbridled free-market capitalism; modern scientific progressivism and New Age spirituality. It was a confused generation that questioned everything and embraced nothing; save the prospect of unimaginable

2. Sara Savage, et al, *Making Sense of Generation Y* (London: Church House Publishing, 2006), p. 6.

technological advancement and the creation of material wealth that technological development so often spawns.

The generation that immediately followed (sometimes known as Generation X), however, soon learned that the unbridled optimism of the previous generation was unfounded. While technology advanced at break-neck speed, it failed to produce the panacea of health, wealth, and happiness expected. The stark reality of AIDS, global economic uncertainty, the rise of militant Islam and the spiritual vacuum left by the wide-spread abandonment of traditional values exposed the previous generation's idealism for the arrogant, intellectually insupportable sham that it was. Sadly, while this generation saw a fleeting return to traditional Christian values, it reverted instead to a combination of moral relativism and postmodernity.

It is against this backdrop that Generation Y has emerged. As Savage, et al note however:

> Generation Y has grown up in a globalized society where many of the limitations of time and space have been overcome by further advances in information and communication technology. In this respect Generation Y is a technological generation that takes computers, emailing, text messaging and the Internet for granted . . . enabl(ing) the further expansion and diversification of popular culture.[3]

The cultural and spiritual effects of this constellation of influences cannot be overstated. Young people today are literally bombarded with information and images unimaginable only a generation ago. Entertainment media are more explicit, more intense, more vivid, more life-like, more imaginative and more accessible than ever before. In addition, every day young people are faced with images of human suffering on a global scale; a 24-hour news cycle that exploits and sensationalises the negative; an apocalyptic vision of everything from the environment to nuclear proliferation; not to mention a virtual network of hundreds of 'friends' (many of whom they have never met, from places they may not be

---

3. Savage, et al, *Making Sense of Generation Y*, p. 7.

able to find on a map) whose influence on their lives and on their thinking are, in many cases, greater than those of their parents, family and classmates.

It is true that in terms of communication, technology is making the world a seemingly smaller place. However, the constant and unrelenting stimulation and overwhelming impact of data, images and information are rendering an entire generation numb to the possibility of contemplation, genuine feeling, and the experience of simply being human. In short, young people's minds as well as their souls are in imminent danger of information over-load.

Making matters worse is the fact that young people today are so poorly equipped to deal with life's so-called big picture issues. Unlike previous generations they are unfamiliar with and/or indifferent to the teachings of Christianity or any other faith tradition. They have instead been led to believe that material existence is a brute fact and that spirituality, transcendent morality, truth and eternal considerations are either inconsequential or blatantly false. Should anyone be surprised then, when the youth of today simply throw in the towel and instead of trying to make sense of their lives and the world around them, choose to escape into the very technological Nirvana that has contributed to their plight? There they can escape (or so it would seem to them) not only the harsh realities of the world around them, but also the reality of their own mortality. By plugging into their iPods, iPhones, iPads, and the like, they seek to escape into their own 'Matrix-like' worlds of pornography, pop-culture and fantasy where reality is whatever they choose to make it. Nothing is actually real and therefore, nothing actually matters. Their actions have no consequences.

Generation Y is not merely a postmodern generation; it is a post-humanist / post-existentialist generation. Like every generation before it, however, these young people desperately need the saving grace of Jesus Christ, 'the way, the truth, and the life' (John 14:6). The Church is indeed at war with the 'principalities, powers, and rulers' (Ephesians 6:12) of this (virtual) world and the stakes are exceedingly high. To the victor will go the spoils—the very souls of this and perhaps future generations of young people.

WHAT YOUNG PEOPLE BELIEVE

As Savage, et al rightly conclude:

> Two things stand out most clearly from recent research conducted in England and Wales on young people's beliefs. First, young people show a great deal of fuzziness and uncertainty concerning traditional Christian beliefs. Yet Christian ideas show a surprising degree of resilience in that they remain in the *background* of young people's minds. Secondly, Christian and other religious or spiritual ideas make little real impact on young people's day-to-day living (apart from times of crisis).[4]

They note that while only 26% of young people recently surveyed reject the notion of God outright (i.e. are atheist) 41% do believe in God and 33% are unsure (i.e. agnostic). When pressed further however, about the nature of the God in whom they do or do not have faith, their lack of understanding and/or appreciation for traditional Christian beliefs becomes more evident. For instance, only 30% believe that Jesus actually rose from the dead (a fundamental Christian doctrine) and only 20% believe in the devil. They tend not to believe in a personal God that is involved in human history, but subscribe instead to a kind of deistic understanding of God; a God who set off the Big Bang, as it were, but who now sits back and watches events from a distance.

These facts should come as no surprise, even to the casual observer, as the decline in Church attendance is well documented and the rise of both secularism and competing faith traditions has diluted the impact of the Christian story on Western culture. However, it is alarming none the less, especially to those who would seek to build a ministry to young people upon a foundation that simply no longer exists.

It is said that generals are always fighting the previous war; perhaps it may also be said that the Church has a tendency to speak to the previous generation? If that is to be avoided, it would be wiser for the Church to worry less about what young people

---

4. Savage, et al, *Making Sense of Generation Y*, p. 19.

don't believe and try instead to understand what they *do* believe and why—thereby establishing a common ground upon which to build a new foundation of understanding.

Space here simply does not permit an exhaustive review of all the literature concerning the beliefs (religious or otherwise) of an entire generation of people in the United Kingdom, the United States or anywhere else. However, the observations of Savage, et al. are very helpful in understanding the impact of popular culture on the religious beliefs of connected young people (i.e. those with access to information technology and exposure to popular music, television and films) in the English-speaking West.

What they observed was a genuine desire among young people to simply find happiness. However, their understanding of happiness was a curious one. As one representative respondent (hypothetically) described it:

> . . . to be happy will be realized through me being my-self, and connecting to others and the universe (without harming them). As I do this, I will create a meaningful and happy life. If we all make this individual effort (everyone's responsibility), each person's happiness will sum into a corporate experience of unity and enjoyment. This happiness is meaningful in itself; it is the Ideal.[5]

Recognizing that theirs is not a Utopian existence however, they foresee both the potential for un-happiness and the availability of resources to help them cope with and ultimately overcome obstacles to happiness, as expressed in the following (hypothetical) statement:

> Bad things can happen in real life that prevent us from attaining . . . happiness . . . But each one of us is surrounded by resources of family and close friends who love us unconditionally. The popular arts provide us with valuable resources: information, choice, creativity. With these, we can experience movement from the Actual (real life where bad things can happen) towards the Ideal (happiness) . . . Having received help, having 'grown' as

5. Savage, et al, *Making Sense of Generation Y*, p. 39.

a result of the meaningful microcosm of family, friends and the popular arts, the happy Ideal that once eluded us is now possible.[6]

The researchers call this paradigm the 'Happy midi-narrative', one that seeks to find fulfilment in the simple pleasures of the here and now; as opposed to the meta-narrative of the Judeo-Christian worldview that operates on an eternal plane. It is neither optimistic nor pessimistic—it is purely pragmatic and utilitarian. Happiness (and by extension morality) is measured on a simple pleasure / pain calculus. There is no ultimate objective or meaning to life, *per se*. Each person merely seeks to increase their own feelings of euphoria while doing no harm to others. This may be accomplished in any way that is deemed to be un-hurtful (to others), including that of absolute escapism. There is no need to embrace or even acknowledge objective reality, so long as one feels happy. God is absent because God is un-necessary (i.e. has no utility) as are sin, guilt, fear of death, final judgement and eternity.

Sadly, in my experience as a university chaplain, this description of what young people believe rings true. Yet the question remains, why do they believe as they do? The answer to that question is far more complex than may be exhausted here, however, as stated previously, if the Church is going to address the religious beliefs of young people today, it must come to grips with the impact of two critical influencers on the formation of those beliefs, namely: postmodernism and New Atheism.

THE EFFECTS OF POSTMODERNISM

As Kieran Flanagan rightly observes in *Postmodernity, Sociology and Religion* (1996):

> Postmodernity is the tag of the times that speaks much of the condition it represents but says little that is memorable. It galvanises to the degree to which it demolishes; it unifies to the degree to which it signifies fragmentation;

6. Savage, et al, *Making Sense of Generation Y*, p. 39.

and it permits any play, but without rules, so that games
seem pointless. Yet postmodernity has its uses. It enables
a theoretical consensus to exist within society that there
is no consensus.[7]

No consensus indeed. In fact, it is fair to say that there is no
consensus among sociologists about postmodernism itself, other
than an acknowledgement of its influence across a wide spectrum
of disciplines. As I see it, postmodernism is to sociology what
quantum theory is to physics. According to quantum mechanics
it is impossible to measure both the position and the momentum
of an object; and some believe that the very process of observation
affects what can be known about a particular object (the 'observer
effect'). However, that doesn't keep physicists from observing,
measuring and drawing conclusions about how things work at the
sub-atomic level. They do the best they can while acknowledging the limits of their current tools and processes. In the case of
examining and understanding postmodernism, we in the social
sciences must undertake a similar task with similar limitations.

Postmodernism similarly acknowledges the limits of language
to accurately describe the deconstructed reality of things. Unfortunately, this has led to the pernicious assumption that because
our knowledge of reality is imperfect, truth (which I define as:
'unconditioned reality') does not itself exist. This is a powerful and
pervasive assumption and is in fact, an epistemological cancer that
threatens not only Christianity but every theological and/or philosophical meta-narrative. The combined effects of both modernism
and postmodernism not only on *what* young people think but *how*
young people think cannot be overstated. They appear to accept
nothing on face value or without critical assessment. They demand
proof (usually as defined by the natural sciences) of every proposition. They are more influenced by their own experiences than by
the testimony of others. They put more credence in the opinion of
their peers than in the opinion of experts. They are slow to accept
the abstract and quick to dismiss whatever seems contrary to their

7. K. Flanagan and P. Jupp, *Postmodernity, Sociology and Religion* (London:
MacMillan Press, 1996), p. 8.

everyday experiences or is counter-intuitive. They are not merely skeptical—they are cynical. Their primary interests are temporal, not eternal and they are resistant to absolutes of any kind.

Needless to say, these predispositions present a considerable challenge to those who would preach the Gospel to young people. Therefore, based upon the assumptions stated above, it seems clear to me that a traditional pedagogical approach to ministry is simply ill suited to the task at hand. We who would minister to young people today should instead be prepared not only to challenge many of the cultural assumptions we encounter, but where appropriate, embrace them as well. We should be prepared to dialogue with young people and to develop both meaningful relationships and opportunities for meaningful spiritual experiences. However, we should also be mindful of the fact that other forces are working against us, including the well equipped, highly intelligent and determined armies of New Atheism.

THE EFFECTS OF NEW ATHEISM / ANTI-THEISM

Atheism is not a new phenomenon—it has always existed. The Bible itself refers to the 'Fool' who 'says in his heart, there is no God' (Psalm 14:1) along with many other references to the faithless and the feckless.

Worldwide, atheists are in a minority position. According to a recent survey conducted by the Encyclopaedia Britannica only 2.3% of respondents identified themselves as atheist with approximately 11% defining themselves as non-religious. In much of the scientifically advanced and economically developed world however the figures are greater with 18% of Europeans declaring themselves to be atheist. The United States is an exception to this rule however, with only 2% of the population claiming to be atheist and 6% agnostic.

As Professor Alister McGrath suggests in his excellent book *The Twilight of Atheism: the Rise and Fall of Disbelief in the Modern World* (2004), these statistics would have come as a complete shock to the post-Enlightenment intelligentsia of the last one hundred and fifty years. They simply assumed that by now the advancement of science would have rendered religious belief obsolete. They expected atheism to have emerged as the self-evident result of scientific inquiry. For most of that time however, faith and unbelief simply co-existed with religious worldviews remaining dominant (despite a period of ascent for atheism in the early modern period). In the late modern period however, as religious belief once again grew in influence and the atheist revolution failed to transpire, a new form of virulent atheism (or anti-theism) emerged that is sometimes referred to as New Atheism.

In his book entitled *The Truth Behind the New Atheism* (2007) David Marshall notes that the New Atheism of Richard Dawkins, Sam Harris, Daniel Dennett, the late Christopher Hitchens and others not only holds that religion and the Abrahamic faiths in particular are false, but that they are 'a curse upon the human race'[8] and should in fact be eradicated. In support of their cause, they present (in various forms and guises) seven basic arguments:

1. Faith is irrational. Faith means 'believing not only without evidence, but in the teeth of evidence', as Dawkins famously put it.

2. Evolution undercuts any reason there may have once been to believe in God (which is why few eminent scientists are religious).

3. Biological and social evolution can explain the origin of religion.

4. The Bible is, at best, a jumbled aggregate of theological cullings that do little to enrich humanity and much to harm us.

5. The Jesus of history was (at best) mortal.

6. Christians in the United States (the 'American Taliban' Dawkins calls them) constitute a profound threat to democracy.

---

8. David Marshall, *The Truth Behind the New Atheism* (Eugene: Harvest House Publishers, 2007), p. 8.

7. All in all, the world would be better off without the Gospel of Jesus Christ, or any religion.[9]

Support for these arguments is quite spurious. Marshall and many others, most notably Professor McGrath in *Dawkins' God* (2005) and *The Dawkins Delusion* (2006) expose their fallacies with considerable effect. However, this particular form of atheism enjoys a certain cache among young people for several reasons:

1. Science and the scientific method are rightly held in high esteem and Dawkins, et al are eminent scientists, thereby adding a presumed credence to their arguments.

2. Dawkins especially has a rapier-like wit and he wields it with great aplomb.

3. They exploit not only the natural skepticism of youth but also the postmodernist tendency to doubt everything and reject absolutist claims (especially truth claims).

4. They often single out and lampoon public figures that profess Christianity in order to discredit it by association.

5. They appeal to young people's natural desire to live carefree lives and explore carnal pleasures and are explicit in their messaging (as evidenced by a recent ad campaign on London buses that read: 'There Probably Isn't a God, So Stop Worrying and Enjoy Your Life').

To a young person with little or no knowledge of Christianity and more importantly, no experience of the transcendent, New Atheism and postmodernity combine to make God little more than a curiosity and Christianity an insignificant relic of the past. It is against this backdrop that the Church must seek to find ways to raise up disciples of Jesus Christ and while it is no easy task, with faith and a little bit of imagination I believe that it can be done.

9. Marshall, *The Truth Behind the New Atheism*, p. 9.

BEING VS. DOING

Mark Yaconelli, co-director of the successful Youth Ministry and Spirituality Project in San Francisco, California compares several different approaches to ministry among young people in his book *Contemplative Youth Ministry* (2006). He defines three popular constructs: 'Content', 'Consumer' and 'Contemplative'.

The first approach (Content) is the one most familiar to the Baby-boomer Generation. It is rooted in the tried and true traditions of one's denomination. It emphasizes teaching and doctrine. It tends to be pedagogical. It essentially attempts to scale down traditional adult ministry methods and then adds a dash of activities to keep the young people interested. There are pros and cons to this approach. On the one hand it doesn't seek to water-down the Gospel message it merely makes it more accessible. On the other hand, as noted earlier, it is built on both sociological and theological foundations that may no longer exist.

The second approach (Consumer) was a knee-jerk reaction to the limitations of the Content approach and was designed to sell Christianity as 'cool' to Generation X. It has its proponents because it can bring young people into contact with the Church. However, not only is the Gospel often watered-down in this scenario, as with any other consumer product it has a limited shelf-life and once young people become bored with what's on offer they are likely to seek something new and improved to satisfy their desires.

The third approach (Contemplative) is an ancient one based on the semi-monastic practices of the early and medieval Church. Here the emphasis is more ontological than sociological and concentrates on what it means to 'be' a Christian and less on 'doing' Christian things. As Mark Yaconelli explains in his book entitled *Contemplative Youth Ministry* (2006):

> There are many ways to describe what is meant by *contemplative*. But in the simplest language, contemplation is 'being' with God within the reality of the present moment. Contemplation is about presence. It's about attentiveness—opening our heart's eye to God, ourselves and others. Contemplation is an attitude of the heart, an

all-embracing hospitality to what is. Contemplation is a natural human disposition—it's the way in which we approach the world as children: vulnerable, open, and awake to the newness of the present moment.[10]

This seems to me to be a very interesting approach as it addresses many of the post-existentialist conditions of Generation Y, stated previously. However, in an ideal situation, we would do well to incorporate elements of the other approaches too, such as: sound biblical teaching and creating appealing settings to create a kind of hybrid of the three approaches. Whatever methods are employed, however, it is clear from all of the research that when ministering to young people, it is absolutely essential that the message, the community and the experiences are all genuine.

GETTING REAL WITH YOUNG PEOPLE

As Syliva Collins-Mayo notes in *The Faith of Generation Y* (2010):

> . . . the faith of Generation Y (is) immanent and this-worldly. It is a faith that members of the generation have in their families, their friends and themselves as they seek to shape their identities authentically in relation to those around them and to their aspirations. What does Jesus Christ have to say to this immanent faith and its various components? In what way is it good news to the Generation Y pictured in this research?[11]

Collins-Mayo cites several things in answer to the questions she poses. Among them are this generation's faith in the power of significant relationships, especially family and close friends. However, all human relationships are unstable and destined to disappoint. Therefore, Collins-Mayo suggests the Church should seek to introduce this generation to a relationship that will never fail them—a relationship with God in Christ that will then further

10. Mark Yaconelli, *Contemplative Youth Ministry* (London: SPCK, 2006), p. 6.

11. Sylvia Collins-Mayo, et al, *The Faith of Generation Y* (London. Church House Publishing, 2010), p. 124.

produce well-grounded, earthly relationships (fellowship) with other Christians.

She rightly suggests that we need to create virtuous circles of relationships. As disciples of Christ we should seek to establish genuine, loving, and committed relationships with young people and in the process introduce them to both the Lord himself and other Christians (the Church). As they begin to grasp the magnitude and the blessings of a relationship with God in Christ, they too will seek to become disciples—and the circles will continue to grow and reproduce.

Of course, this kind of discipleship comes at a cost. It requires time, energy, love, commitment, and a willingness to be open, honest, and vulnerable. It can be an exhausting enterprise, and it may not always produce the fruits for which we hope. It is however exactly how Jesus discipled his first followers and it seems to me to be a very good paradigm to follow with Generation Y. In order to be effective however, we who seek to make disciples in this way must always practice what we preach.

APOLOGETICS IN PRAXIS

The Oxford Dictionary of the Christian Church defines apologetics as, 'the defence of the Christian faith on intellectual grounds by trained theologians and philosophers'. Professor Alister McGrath in his book entitled *Bridge Building, Effective Christian Apologetics* (1992) states that, 'in its basic sense, it is an apologia for the Christian faith—a presentation and defence of its claims to truth and relevance in the great marketplace of ideas'.[12] Both of these definitions are of course true, however in order to win people's hearts as well as their minds, we should always make apologetics more than just an intellectual exercise—we should make it a way of life.

Collins-Mayo suggests that we live out our apologetics in seven key areas:

---

12. Alister McGrath, *Bridge Building: Effective Christian Apologetics* (Leicester: Intervarsity Press, 1992), p. 9.

1. Community—'The Christian vision for humanity is for a Church where all people relate to each other in the name of Christ (ref. Galatians 3:28) and live out the story of God's forgiving love from one generation to the next'.

2. Family—'. . . a primary resource that the Church can offer to young people is the opportunity for them to build nurturing relationships with adults'.

3. Character—'(the) interplay between private and public practice'.

4. Location—'the Internet has not rendered obsolete the relationship between 'place' and religious experience'.

5. Sacralized Youth Work—'Sacralized youth work provides places for young people to take part in ritual with sacred connotations, and/or interact with symbols with a sacred meaning'.

6. Ethics and Authenticity—'(to) provide an example of what a life of faith might look like'.

7. Authentic Church—'. . . while not necessarily involved with the Church . . . young people appreciate its role in society . . . particularly so at points of difficulty and need when young people . . . look to the Church to provide them with a point of reference'.[13]

All of the above reminds me of advice given at my ordination by my friend and mentor Dr John Wesley Smith—'most people' (especially young people?), he said, 'would rather *see* a good sermon than *hear* one' and of course he was absolutely correct. Students especially, who spend much of their time sitting in lectures, don't want yet another lecture about God. If God exists, they prefer to see evidence of God's existence in the lives of genuine believers.

In the next chapter I will discuss how we tried to apply these lessons to our ministries at Oxford University, however, it should be noted that while Oxford is a unique environment in which to

13. Sylvia Collins-Mayo, et al, *The Faith of Generation Y* (London. Church House Publishing, 2010), p. 110–16.

serve, the frames of reference cited above are everywhere to be found; and the challenges they present to faith leaders are the same for pastors, parents, youth leaders, teachers, counselors, fellow parishioners and chaplains alike.

3

Graduate Ministry at Oxford University

As mentioned previously, I have been involved in and/or worked alongside, several organizations that are designed to meet the spiritual needs of graduate students at Oxford University. While the unique setting of Oxford and the specific needs of graduate students present certain challenges, I believe the lessons learned from these ministries are universally applicable for anyone ministering to Generation Y and therefore warrant closer examination, starting with the aforementioned Oxford Evangelical Pastorate.

A BRIEF HISTORY OF THE OXFORD EVANGELICAL PASTORATE

When a person enters the chapel of an Oxford college, such as the one at New College, they enter more than a church building; they enter the mysterious and often bewildering world of the British Establishment. The college's official name is the College of St. Mary, however at the time of its inception in 1379 A.D. nearby Oriel College was also known as the College of St. Mary. So as not to confuse the two, the latter became known as the New College of

St. Mary and over time, simply New College. Since the 15th Century it has enjoyed an association with some of the most important educational institutions in the country, including Eton College and King's College, Cambridge where future kings and prime ministers have been trained for centuries. It is a place where 'the great and the good' have sent their children to receive a world-class education, network with other privileged heirs and become steeped in the deep-seeded traditions of both church and state.

As with many British institutions of higher learning, it has a long association with the Church of England. Originally a training college for priests, the centre of the College is its magnificent chapel, a medieval masterpiece adorned by the artwork of Epstein and El Greco, a forty-foot high rood screen and a world-renowned choir. It is also the official seat of the college chaplain and during term-time it serves as the spiritual and ceremonial centre of college life; and in that, it is not unique. Of the forty-four colleges and permanent private halls, approximately thirty of them have chapels similar to the chapel at New College. Some, such as the cathedral at Christ Church (which doubles as a college chapel and a diocesan cathedral) are even grander than New College Chapel and most are rooted in the high church traditions of traditional Anglicanism (i.e. Book of Common Prayer) or the Anglo-Catholicism of John Henry Newman's 19th Century Oxford Movement.

There are however, some exceptions to this rule and ever since the emergence of 18th Century Methodism there has been a strong vein of evangelicalism at work within the University. St. Edmund's Hall, Jesus College, St. Peter's College and Wycliffe Hall all have evangelical associations. However, the most prominent evangelical ministry to the students at Oxford University is undoubtedly the Oxford Evangelical Pastorate.

The Pastorate was originally conceived as a counter to the influence of certain unbelieving scholars on the lives of younger, impressionable undergraduates. While technically an 'unofficial' ministry at first, the Oxford Pastorate eventually became recognized by both the Oxford Diocese and the University, thanks in large part to the association of respected scholars, such as C.S.

Lewis and others. That said, it has always operated outside the collegiate system; and consequently the Pastorate has been viewed by some college chaplains with a certain degree of suspicion and skepticism. The skepticism of some college chaplains notwithstanding however, the Pastorate was quite effective in offering students (primarily undergraduates at first) an evangelical alternative to college chapel services. This was especially true when the Pastorate became integrated with the ministry of St. Aldates Church, a large and prominent evangelical congregation in the city centre. Students flocked to St. Aldates to hear the preaching of notable pastors, such as Michael Green and to experience contemporary forms of worship. However, in recent years two phenomena have emerged that have caused the Council and the Trustees of the Oxford Evangelical Pastorate to re-cast its vision for ministry. They are:

1. The emergence of several evangelical congregations within the City offering various opportunities for contemporary worship and sound preaching.

2. The dramatic shift in the demographics of the University from primarily British undergraduates to a large influx of international graduate students.

The change in demographics was of particular interest to the Council and the Trustees. They recognized that the center of a graduate student's life was not their college, but their department, their laboratory or their faculty library. They sensed that graduate life could be a very lonely existence, especially for international students and that graduate students were in residence for everything from one term to five years and that these factors could make it difficult for them to establish meaningful relationships. They also realised that many of them come from countries where Christianity is either unknown or suppressed and that a unique opportunity existed for the Church in Oxford to impact the Church globally; and so they decided to shift their focus from undergraduates to graduate students and reformed the Pastorate accordingly.

The Pastorate was embarking on a totally new endeavour. This meant that whomever they chose to lead this ministry would have to do more than merely provide an alternative to the University's collegiate system, he/she would have to create a totally new collegiate system of religious professionals from both within and outside the University. He/she would have to provide genuine leadership from among a team of peers, yet do so without the authority of an official university or ecclesiastical office. In order to pull this off and in order to overcome the problems inherent in starting anything from scratch (not to mention having to navigate through the potential minefields of latent suspicion, skepticism and parochialism), the new chaplain would need to possess exceptional gifts for ministry.

Having observed the work of the person appointed, Revd. Dr. Jonathan Brant, I can say with confidence that he has not only succeeded in fulfilling the expectations of the Council and the Trustees, he has done so with considerable patience and grace. In fact, I would say that of all his many gifts, his greatest gift and the one that I would commend to anyone seeking to minister to Generation Y, is what I and many others, cited below, would call: grace-centred leadership.

GRACE-CENTRED LEADERSHIP

What is meant by the term 'grace-centred leadership'? In my view, grace-centred leadership may best be described as humble leadership. That is to say it is leadership that is rooted not only in our nature as fallen human beings, but in our knowledge that we are fallen yet forgiven; weak yet empowered; unlovable yet loved; broken yet healed; sinful yet sanctified; afraid yet courageous; lonely yet not alone; unworthy yet called; leaders yet servants—servants not only of those whom we lead, but ultimately, servants of God.

As Professor Sean Lucas notes, grace-centred leadership is founded upon:

... two framing principles: grace-centred leadership starts with what God says is true about us—both by nature and grace—and moves to particular practices of leading. Grace-centred leadership recognizes that our relationships with those whom we lead must ground and guide the results we seek to achieve.[1]

Dan Allender in his book entitled *Leading with a Limp* (2006) puts it this way:

The ironic truth that those who proclaim the Gospel need it more than those who hear it is not new. It just isn't being said loudly and clearly enough in this day of spin and professionalism and big programs. These days need certain stories to be told again and again. We need to tell stories about failure and the need for grace; we need to share stories that invite the hearer to consider the wild, inverted paradox of grace. In fact, these three great paradoxes need to be told often: the already and the not yet, the call to be strong and tender, and the ways of being wise as a serpent and innocent as a dove.[2]

Embracing the concept of grace-centred leadership requires a journey of self-discovery. It requires leaders to understand who they are as human beings as well as Christians; it involves discovering who we are as God has made us and who we are as fallen human beings, both in that which is common to all people and that which is unique to ourselves. This requires us to consider all of the influences on our lives from our childhoods to the present day. Leaders must be honest with themselves about what it is that makes them tick. They need to consider the values they imbibed as children growing up in a particular household, in a particular culture and at a particular time in history. This would include the negative influences as well as the positive influences as they all contribute to who we are as people and therefore as leaders.

1. Sean Lucas, *Grace-Centered Leadership*. Reformed Theological Seminary Lectures. Jackson, MS. Delivered January 10-14, 2011.

2. Dan Allender, *Leading With a Limp* (Colorado Springs: Waterbrook Press, 2006), pp. 176-77.

When I was a younger man, I loved to read the biographies of great men and women and in doing so, came to appreciate how our formative years influence how we think, the values we hold dear and the motivation behind our actions. For example, when I read the exhaustive biography of Sir Winston Churchill by Martin Gilbert (2000) I was struck by the fact that this icon of the 20th Century was in fact a very Victorian man. I was also struck by the complex relationships he had with his parents and how their influences not only shaped whom he was as a person but motivated him to lead and to succeed.

For Christian leaders however, it is equally important that we understand who *we* are in Christ. We need to appreciate the lordship of Christ in our lives, without succumbing to a kind of experiential moralism that ultimately leads to both pride and prejudice. We need to avoid the mistake of the Pharisees, for instance, which confused outward expressions of devotion and contempt for those (apparently) less righteous than themselves with a genuine devotion to God. This can only be avoided however, if we maintain an ever-present knowledge of our own need for grace in Jesus Christ.

This was a theme that drove the German theologian and Christian martyr Dietrich Bonhoeffer throughout his brief but exceptional life. As his biographer, Eric Metaxas put it in *Bonhoeffer, Pastor, Martyr, Prophet, Spy* (2010):

> A major theme for Bonhoeffer was that every Christian must be 'fully human' by bringing God into his whole life, not merely into some spiritual realm. To be an ethereal figure that merely talked about God but somehow refused to get his hands dirty in the real world, in which God had placed him, was bad theology. Through Christ, God had shown that he meant us to be in this world and to obey him with our actions in this world. So Bonhoeffer would get his hands dirty, not because he had grown impatient, but because God was speaking to him about further steps of obedience.[3]

---

3. Eric Metaxas, *Bonhoeffer: Pastor, Martyr, Prophet, Spy* (Nashville: Thomas Nelson. 2010–Kindle edition.

Obedience of course, is central to grace-centred leadership; obedience not to a set of rules, but obedience to God's command that we love one another as he has loved us. This is central to the entire proposition. As the Apostle John teaches us, we should love others because God has first loved us and just as it is in God's very nature to love, so it must become second nature for us, as disciples of Jesus Christ, to love, not merely as an emotion, but love in action; rooted in our very sense of mission (i.e. to build God's Kingdom on earth).

Building God's kingdom however is not done in isolation. Citing the models given to us by the Apostle Paul in Ephesians 4 and 1 Corinthians 12, Sean Lucas reminds us that the Body of Christ is a 'complex system' of different yet interdependent parts, each with a role to play in being the Church. As leaders we must not merely recognize the part that we ourselves play, but must seek to bring out the best in those whom we lead as well; to ensure the entire body is healthy and functioning according to God's will and to God's glory.[4]

Sociologist Stephen Covey, in his seminal work entitled *Principle-centered Leadership* (1990) would seem to agree with this sentiment when he says:

> The place to begin any relationship is inside ourselves, inside our circle of influence, our own character. As we become independent—proactive, centred in correct principles, value-driven, and able to organize and execute around priorities in our life with integrity—we can choose to become interdependent: capable of building rich, enduring, productive relationships with other people.[5]

I don't think we can overstate the fact that how one does mission is just as important as what one accomplishes. It is extremely easy for those of us who are in leadership positions to become so goal oriented that we seek quantitative results, when God's

4. Lucas, *Grace-Centered Leadership*.

5. Stephen R. Covey, *Principle-Centered Leadership* (New York: Fireside, 1990), p. 60.

measurements are often more qualitative in nature. Ignoring this fact is very dangerous, in that it may cause us to forget the feelings and needs of the people with whom we work; sacrificing their emotions on the altar of our efficiency. In other words, we may be tempted to opt for quick wins (obvious, short-term successes) instead of seeking the genuine transformation of individuals and churches. However, I believe that we are called to take the higher road and work toward transformation, even though there will be times when things do not go smoothly. To do so requires maturity, tact, and exceptional communications skills, not to mention a high degree of personal humility, patience, and prayer. Leadership can be a difficult business, but it is also essential to our task; and it is a mantle that God chooses to bestow on some of his children for his purposes and according to his divine will. Christian leaders may take comfort in the fact that we are doing God's will and if we remain faithful and obedient, God will always equip, sustain and empower us in our work for the Kingdom.

As I will examine in more detail below, Dr. Brant possesses the qualities associated with grace-centred leadership in abundance, the result of which has been a transformed and transformational ministry. A closer look both at what he has done and how he has done it; should be beneficial to us all.

As noted earlier, I have been more than a casual observer of the Pastorate. In order to truly understand why it works as well as it does however, I personally embarked on the collection and analysis of a large amount of what researchers call 'qualitative data'. This included direct observation of the Chaplain in action, a review of pertinent documents relating to the Pastorate and an extensive interview of Dr. Brant himself. I then collated the data and compared it to models found in the existing literature, with special attention given to the grace-centred leadership model discussed above, as well as my own experience as a fellow chaplain in Oxford. The results produced the case study found below, including the development of a pattern for ministry that I call, 'The Ten Cs of Missional Leadership'.

THE OXFORD EVANGELICAL PASTORATE: CASE STUDY

Reverend Doctor Jonathan Brant assumed the position of Oxford Evangelical Pastorate Chaplain at a commissioning service conducted by the Bishop of Oxford on November 7, 2008 at St. Andrew's Church, Oxford. The service itself was interesting in that it sent several mixed messages to the local Christian community and to the University. In the first place, Dr. Brant was not an ordained clergyperson at the time and was therefore not under the direct episcopal care of the Bishop of Oxford. The Pastorate, while recognized by the diocese is overseen by an independent Council and Board of Trustees and is not an official ministry of the Oxford Diocese. Secondly, when the invitations for the commissioning service were sent out, they referred to the chaplain as having responsibility for the spiritual nurture of graduate students at the University. That is simply incorrect. Under the collegiate system, which is based upon the Church of England's parochial system, it is still the college chaplains who are 'officially' responsible for the 'cure of souls' within the University. Lastly, the Pastorate had a long association with St. Aldates Church and while there was clearly a desire to make a break with the past, having the service in another church, may have been perceived by some as a snub to St. Aldates, which had hosted the Pastorate for most of its history. It was an inauspicious start to say the least.

The rocky start not withstanding however, the Oxford Evangelical Pastorate has in fact succeeded in breaking new ground in its mission to minister to graduate students and to be a missional community to the University at large. It has accomplished this by being effective in several areas.

Firstly, it has created an organizational structure that is flexible and fluid. In addition to the chaplain, there is an associate chaplain (who is ordained) as well as two, student lay assistants and ten, student mission associates. They meet regularly to pray and to plan their work among the graduate community and in their outreach to the University at large.

Secondly, it has created an effective network of fellow practitioners from across the University, local churches and other para-church ministries who meet regularly to pray for each other's work, to share information and to seek opportunities for cooperation and synergy.

Thirdly, it has established relationships with Christian faculty members who are willing to share their personal experiences as Christian academics working in a secular (and sometimes hostile) setting. It has also established its own credentials as a research centre within the University and begun to work across disciplines on issues relating to character and ethical leadership.

Fourthly, it has taken a leadership role in the communication of ministry opportunities and events throughout the University and the city and supports many of those opportunities and events with resources, manpower, and prayer. It also sponsors many events of its own from speaker forums to informal lunches and even the occasional worship event.

Fifthly, it has created a community of believers without creating a 'cult' within the University or a congregation that competes with existing local churches.

Lastly, it provides pastoral care and support for students in need.

In all of these things, a pattern of grace-centred leadership has emerged that I call the 'Ten Cs of Missional Leadership'.

TEN CS OF MISSIONAL LEADERSHIP

1. Christ-Centeredness: As the original charter stated back in 1893, the primary role of the Pastorate Chaplain is 'to take up the spiritual side of the ideal Tutor's work, and through frequent and affectionate intercourse, to seek to win to Christ . . . (a) large number of University men . . .' In short, the mission of the Pastorate has always been to preach, teach and share through daily activities and fellowship the saving power of God in Jesus Christ and that is still its primary focus today. However, while the original vision saw the role as an extension of one's academic responsibilities (i.e. 'Tutor's

work'), the emphasis today is on a Christian witness that is more organic and more peer oriented. What hasn't changed however, is the emphasis on 'frequent and affectionate intercourse.' When I asked what first attracted him to this new role, the Chaplain shared with me his desire to integrate his personal experience as a scholar (i.e. a recent graduate student himself) with his call to Christian ministry. By reaching out to graduate students who are experiencing many of the same pressures, doubts, questions, fears, etc. that the Chaplain himself experienced as a student only recently, there is an opportunity to share the grace of Christ in a way that is open, honest, relevant, vulnerable and relational. As Dan Allender notes:

> . . . a leader must first walk into his own narrative. If he plunges into his own story, then he will understand better where he refuses to live with faith, hope and love. He will better be able to name how he attempts to make truth serve his own idolatry rather than allowing the lies of his life to be exposed by the searing goodness of God. We lead others to God only to the degree that we are aware of how much we flee him, how little we truly desire him, and yet how God is also the deepest, truest, and sweetest desire of our hearts.[6]

2. Courage: Willing to be open, honest, and vulnerable enough to make an impact on the lives of skeptical students is a courageous thing to do, but it is essential if one is going to reach a postmodern audience. It would appear the Pastorate Chaplain and his team are willing to take the risks inherent in telling their stories, because they know that their stories are real and that their experiences of God's love and grace are real; and that telling those stories may have a positive impact on those whom they seek to reach with the Gospel of Jesus Christ. To be real with students however, one must be humble, not haughty and in an institution where a premium is placed on excellence and where failure is feared more than anything else, it takes courage to be humble. As Allender states quite emphatically:

---

6. Allender, *Leading With a Limp*, p. 161.

No one is humble by nature . . . Humility comes from humiliation, not from the choice to be self-effacing or a strong urge to give others credit. Humility that has not come from suffering due to one's own arrogance is either a pragmatic strategy to get along with others or a natural predilection that seems to befit only a few rare individuals. For most leaders, humility comes only by wounds suffered from foolish falls. This is the terrible secret about leadership and life: we achieve brokenness by falling off our throne. To be broken is not a choice; it is a gift . . . to experience brokenness and humiliation, all you have to do is lead.[7]

3. Character: The Oxford Evangelical Pastorate seeks not only to foster the development of character, but also to exhibit character in the lives of the chaplains and the student associates. That means challenging and even rebuking the popular notion that there is a distinction to be made between the sacred and the secular elements of one's life. As Allender rightly observes:

The purpose of life is to present every person mature in Christ. Each human being is meant to become like Jesus—and to mark other lives with a beauty that draws them to Jesus. The scope of that calling is so enormous as to be beyond comprehension. It means subsuming every dimension of life . . .[8]

Consequently, many of the programs and events designed by or supported by the Pastorate have something to do with the integration of one's spiritual life (and faith) with their academic discipline. One example is a course offered through the University and co-sponsored by the Pastorate entitled 'Developing a Christian Mind'. The brainchild of Professor Donald Hay, formerly Pro-vice Chancellor of the University, the course seeks to counter the prevalence of radical materialism and secularism with a Christian world-view that encompasses every aspect of one's life. The course brings together some of the greatest thought-leaders in

---

7. Allender, *Leading With a Limp*, p. 70.
8. Allender, *Leading With a Limp*, p. 144.

their respective fields of science, medicine, law, theology, etc., all of whom are also committed Christians. Over the course of a term or a weekend away, students are encouraged to consider what it means to be truly human and in the process, what it means to be a person of exceptional character. Out of this course developed an inter-disciplinary research project known as the Oxford Character Project that includes a mentoring program called the Global Leadership Initiative, of which I was a part. Together these programs help students develop the knowledge and skills necessary for effective and faithful leadership.

4. Collegiality: While the Pastorate operates outside the traditional collegiate system, one of the first things the new chaplain sought to do was to create a new collegiality among his fellow practitioners both within the University and outside the University. Those working within the University included the college chaplains who did not feel particularly threatened by the work of the Pastorate. Many recognized the fact that graduate students don't share the same rhythm of the terms that undergraduates enjoy and around which the college chaplains plan their events. Others recognized that some of the colleges (especially the graduate only colleges such as Kellogg College, St. Anthony's College, Wolfson College, etc.) don't have chapels or chaplains at all and were happy to offer their services to graduate students where appropriate. He was also keen to work closely with the Graduate Christian Union (a student organization that is officially recognized by the University). Among those organizations outside the University, but with ministries directed toward students, he sought to work closely with the Oxford American Mission, Friends International, the Veritas Forum, the Trinity Forum and other like-minded ministries. Lastly, he was especially keen to work with pastoral staff from the large city churches, such as St. Aldates, St. Ebbe's, and St. Andrew's, whose focus is on graduate student ministry. When I asked him how he managed to create such a collegiate environment, especially when he lacks any official university or ecclesiastical office, he replied that it was a combination of two things: personality and trust. The former is merely a reflection of the chaplain's demeanour

as a gentle and non-threatening man. There is little he could do to affect it one way or the other. The latter however is a reflection of his own character as a man of God and that is the result of both his desire and ability to be a person of integrity as well as the grace of God that has gifted him in this way.

5. Commonality of Purpose: In the introduction to their book entitled *Leadership on the Line* (2002) Heifetz and Lansky make the following statement:

> Leadership is worth the risk because the goals extend beyond material gain or personal advancement. By making the lives of people around you better, leadership provides meaning in life. It creates purpose.[9]

I believe that is exactly what the Pastorate is trying to do with its ministry to graduate students and its mission to the wider University. It is trying to instil in students a sense that what they are doing is important because it is part of a much bigger plan—it is part of God's plan for their lives and for all of creation. Their value as students, scholars, people, etc., isn't dependent upon the accolades they receive or the papers they publish or even their own sense of self-satisfaction. Their value as human beings is based upon a series of relationships that transcend anything remotely related to their success at university. Their value as human beings and their ultimate purpose in life is directly related to their relationship with God and the relationships they form with every other human being whose lives they touch. If there is a single message that everyone who works in student ministry seeks to communicate above everything else it is simply this: ' . . . seek first his kingdom and his righteousness, and all these things will be given to you as well' (Matthew 6:33).

6. Catalytic Mission: When I asked the chaplain what the most significant difference was between the former model of ministry employed by the Pastorate and the new model, he said that is was a newly found emphasis on catalytic mission. That is to say, in the

9. Heifetz, R. and M. Linsky, *Leadership on the Line: staying alive through the dangers of leading* (Boston. Harvard Business School Press, 2002–Kindle edition.

past, the chaplains were hired to do ministry among the students. Now, however, the emphasis is on raising up an entire generation of students to be ministers themselves among their fellow students. Hence the creation of the mission associate positions—students who are committed Christians and who with proper training, direction and mentoring can become ambassadors of Christ within their colleges, their departments, their laboratories and in their residences.

7. Corporate Mission: When I asked him what he would like his legacy to be, the chaplain replied that he would like to be remembered for creating a corporate mission among all those who seek to bring the Gospel of Jesus Christ to the University of Oxford and its students. I once shared with Dr. Brant my belief that ministering to students is like 'ministering to a parade' (an expression once used by the pastor of an expat community in a large cosmopolitan city). He agreed, and noted that it is very difficult to keep up with their busy lives and the complex network of events and associations that mark their time at university. However, if one can create a ministry that incorporates all of the resources available from within the University and the Church, the ability to remain in contact with each student increases exponentially. To accomplish this task however requires the establishment of trusting relationships that are both deep and wide. They must be deep enough to withstand the pressures of external influences that may or may not be of sinister intent; and they must be wide enough to cover an entire spectrum of possible needs. As Covey rightly notes:

> For the leader who wishes to increase principle-centred power, a long-term commitment is required. Trust in relationships, which is the foundation of principle-centred power, cannot be fabricated ad hoc. Sincerity cannot be faked for long. Eventually leaders reveal themselves. And what a leader is, beyond what a leader can do to or for his followers, ultimately determines the depth of principle-centred power.[10]

10. Covey, *Principle-Centered Leadership*, p. 105.

8. Care and Counsel: All Christian ministries regardless of their pedigrees or emphases ultimately involve the provision of pastoral care and counsel. In fact, it is virtually impossible to be a genuine community without the willingness to care for each other in times of need and the Pastorate is no exception. As Allender states rather sublimely:

> Honesty with truth fosters a community of care. The more honest I am with you about my alien life, the more possible it is for you to suffer with me and delight in me. I am an alien because I am not at home. At this point I am also an alien to the world that is to come. So I am at home nowhere—an alien to both heaven and earth. But that's okay because it is not possible to feel pain for someone who is not an alien and a stranger . . . Being cared for means that leaders must reveal their own suffering, so that others can enter the war that is in their hearts . . . Care gives and receives both sorrow and delight . . . A leadership team is meant to be a community of friends who suffer and delight in one another.[11]

The Pastorate is a community of friends both within itself and to the University as a whole and its ministry is to fellow 'aliens'.

9. Communication: Good communication is critical to anyone in a leadership role, but it is especially important to those who seek consensus where there are genuine ideological differences. Such is the case for the Oxford Evangelical Pastorate. Its roots are clearly in the Reformed / Evangelical traditions of the 19th Century, yet it often finds itself holding common ground with Liberals and Roman Catholics against the forces of postmodern secularism, radical atheism and many other anti-Christian movements. So how do they remain true to their heritage without becoming isolated within the wider Christian community? How do they engage with the wider community without upsetting their primary constituents? The answer lies in good communication and the key to good communication is the timely transmission of accurate information. It is that simple. Volumes have been written about the

11. Covey, *Principle-Centered Leadership*, pp. 122-23.

art of good communication, but at the end of the day there is no substitute for telling people what they need to know, when they need to know it. Contrary to popular opinion however, it would seem from the example of the Pastorate Chaplain that good communication isn't about spin but about honesty and integrity. When the Bishop's letter of invitation to the chaplain's commissioning caused a stir among some college chaplains, there was no attempt to smooth things over. On the contrary, there was a simple admission that mistakes had been made and forgiveness requested. Sometimes the most important thing to communicate is a simple *mea culpa.*

10. Creativity: Lastly, the Oxford Evangelical Pastorate has demonstrated missional leadership in its willingness not to seek control over every situation, but to trust God and to be creative in its response to the things it cannot control. As Allender says:

> The more complex the situation, the more we tend to resort to analysis . . . But chaos theory reminds us that every effort to measure, let alone control, a phenomenon not only changes it but moves it in an unpredictable direction. Control is the province of idiots . . . Imagine living out the belief that creativity finds its best soil in the dirt of chaos . . . The process of chaos-induced creativity invites us to surrender to the God who honors all creativity with new chaos and, with it, opportunities to re-create again and again.[12]

The Oxford Evangelical Pastorate recently seized the opportunity to re-create itself after one hundred and twenty years. Thankfully for all those who are under its influence, it is blessed with grace-centred, missional leaders who seek not to build kingdoms of their own, but seek only to build the Kingdom of God—at Oxford University and wherever God chooses to plant those who have come to know God's Son through its ministry.

It is important for readers to realize that, other than its unusual setting, there is nothing particularly unique about the Oxford Evangelical Pastorate. All of the principles described above

12. Allender, *Leading With a Limp,* pp. 91-93.

may be applied to any ministry anywhere, but for all of the reasons highlighted earlier, they will have particular appeal to the people of Generation Y.

OXFORD UNIVERSITY GRADUATE CHRISTIAN UNION: CASE STUDY

Another important ministry to graduate students at Oxford University is the Graduate Christian Union (GCU), started by Rev. Joe Martin (to whom I dedicated this book). The GCU grew out of a merger between two similar organizations, the Graduate Christian Forum (GCF) and the Graduate Christian Network (GCN). While somewhat different in emphasis (the GCF was more interested in intellectual pursuits while the GCN focused on Christian fellowship), they shared a common vision; specifically to help graduate students integrate their Christian beliefs with their academic lives. Since 2001 it has been an officially recognized society of Oxford University and while it has no denominational affiliation, its origins are clearly rooted in the evangelical tradition of the Church of England. Its original Constitution was based on the doctrinal standards of an organization known as The International Fellowship of Evangelical Students. More recently however, the GCU decided to broaden its appeal and now uses one of the most commonly professed of the ecumenical creeds—the Nicene Creed.

Theological uniformity however, is not the GCU's primary concern. Instead, the GCU seeks first and foremost to be a conversational community, where people of all faiths and none can come together and explore Christianity's truth claims. It is purposeful in its desire to critically engage other worldviews in the marketplace of ideas and in the process reaffirm the basic tenets of the Christian faith. It seeks the development of Christian minds and regularly invites speakers from across the University's varied faculties to discuss the relationship between intellectual inquiry and religious belief.

The ways in which the GCU functions as a Christian community are simple. They include a series of events that occur uniquely once per calendar year such as their participation in Freshers' Week at the beginning of Michaelmas Term and the Annual General Meeting. Then there are events that occur regularly at the start of each new term, such as a start of term worship event and/or a special guest lecture designed to engage with people from outside the GCU and/or the Christian community at large.

The GCU also sponsors regular weekly events during term, including a regular series of talks given by Christian academics on the integration of one's faith and academic discipline. Then there are a series of annual events that are co-sponsored with other student-centered Christian ministries, such as the International Student Welcome, the Veritas Forum, the Trinity Forum, the Oxford University Christian Mind Course and the UK Graduate Christian Conference.

Lastly there are regular spontaneous fellowship events that occur throughout the year, especially in-between terms when undergraduates leave the city and graduate students find themselves on their own. These events may be anything from small prayer groups to dinners with Council members to evenings at the movies. They differ in kind but are all designed to foster community while offering a Christian alternative to other more common social activities available to lonely students.

As a student-led organization that is officially recognized by the University, the GCU is the nucleus around which all other graduate ministries revolve, including the Oxford American Mission, a ministry to American Expats that I founded in 2006, whose mission, vision and ministry principles are discussed in detail below.

OXFORD AMERICAN MISSION: CASE STUDY

It would be absurd to pretend that my approach to ministry isn't impacted by my many years in the corporate world, but I don't happen to subscribe to the notion that churches or ministries should be run more like businesses (as many people suggest). I do however believe that churches and ministries can learn from the things that businesses do best. In my experience, successful companies always establish clear and concise goals and the first step in that process is the development of simply stated vision and mission statements.

Vision Statement of the Oxford American Mission

The Oxford American Mission is a fellowship of American scholars, their families and friends who seek to encounter God in Christ; explore His Word; equip new leaders and encourage one another to build God's kingdom in the University and beyond, in a humble spirit of faith, hope and love.

This is a simple affirmation of what the ministry is. Next, is the OAM mission statement that explains what it seeks to do.

Mission Statement of the Oxford American Mission

The Oxford American Mission seeks to do the following:

1. Promote the reading and study of the Bible.

2. Provide pastoral care and counseling to students in need of such services.

3. Encourage students to consider the truth claims of the Christian faith as compared to the truth claims of the culture around them (i.e. apologetics).

4. Promote the integration of faith and study/work.

5. Provide a place of culturally sensitive Christian fellowship (and occasional worship).

6. Promote involvement in the life of the local church.

7. Work closely with other University-based Christian organizations (i.e. Friends International; O.I.C.C.U.; OEP; GCU) to equip future leaders with Christian beliefs and values.

8. Work closely with other International Christian organizations (i.e. Trinity Forum; Veritas Forum) to equip future leaders with Christian beliefs and values.

Ministry Principles of the Oxford American Mission

The Oxford American Mission is based upon the following biblical principles:

1. ' . . . all have sinned and fall short of the glory of God' (Romans 3:23).

2. ' . . . God so loved the world that He gave His only son, that whoever believes in Him shall not perish but have eternal life' (John 3:16).

3. ' . . . All Scripture is God-breathed and is useful for teaching, rebuking, correcting and training in righteousness' (2 Timothy 3:16).

4. ' . . . The fear of the LORD is the beginning of knowledge, but fools despise wisdom and discipline' (Proverbs 1:7).

5. ' . . . He that ruleth over men must be just, ruling in the fear of God' (2 Samuel 23:2).

6. ' . . . where there is no vision, the people perish' (Proverbs 29:18).

7. ' . . . if we walk in the light, as he is in the light, we have fellowship with one another, and the blood of Jesus, his Son, purifies us from all sin' (1 John 1:17).

The visions, missions and principles (i.e. values) of the Oxford American Mission, the GCU and the Pastorate weren't created in a vacuum; they were born of deep theological reflection and many years of Christian ministry. They reflect what I believe to be the central tenets of any ministry, but especially those designed specifically to meet the spiritual needs of Generation Y. What makes them somewhat unique is their university setting, but again, the emphasis on integrating one's faith with one's work and the desire to seek the truth are universally applicable.

LOVING GOD WITH ONE'S MIND

Working in a university setting, provides a constant reminder that the Gospel of Jesus Christ is competing with a myriad of other belief systems in the aforementioned 'marketplace of ideas'. One of the great scandals of late modern evangelicalism has been a tendency to undermine the value of higher education and a well-documented anti-intellectualism. This is unfortunate, unnecessary, and simply unacceptable in a university setting, but in my opinion, no less scandalous in any other setting, including local parishes. It is true that many of the students with whom we engage are hoping to become career academics; however, instead of perpetuating the myth that intellectualism and faith are somehow incompatible, these ministries are dedicated to helping students integrate their faith with every other aspect of their lives and that is what good discipleship is all about.

COME, LET US REASON TOGETHER

Of all the un-truths told by Dawkins, Harris, Dennett and the other anti-theists one of the most shocking is the notion that all faith is 'blind faith'. It is true that 'faith precedes understanding', but *faith does not preclude thinking*. Faith in God and in Jesus is a perfectly reasonable proposition and while the decision to become a believer is ultimately a spiritual one, it none the less involves a conscious decision whether or not to accept or reject Christianity's truth claims. To that end, while in Oxford, one of the student leaders and I developed two, weekly discussion groups, aimed at exploring the reasonableness of Christianity.

The first was a mid-week apologetics group designed to help Christian students defend the faith against the false accusations of the anti-theists. Each week a new area of contention was addressed, such as: 'Can the existence of God be proven?'; 'Are the Scriptures reliable?'; 'Are human beings merely biological machines?'; 'Are evolution and creation incompatible?'; 'Is morality without God possible?'; etc. The purpose of the group was not to provide pat answers, but to help Christian students think critically about their beliefs and to develop the tools necessary to defend those beliefs intelligently.

The second group was a Saturday morning workshop involving both Christians and non-Christians (and was in fact co-sponsored by the University Secular Society) that I had inherited from a previous chaplain who had gone on to do parish ministry. This group met to read and discuss the works of well-known Christian thinkers (such as Sören Kierkegaard or C.S. Lewis). The purpose of the group was three-fold:

1. To get students to think about big-picture issues.

2. To demonstrate the intellectual veracity of Christianity.

3. To reach out to and establish relationships with non-believers (what some people might call 'pre-evangelism').

These two groups became regular fixtures for their participants and were instrumental in helping several students re-examine their understanding of Christianity. Whether they ultimately led to anyone becoming a believer or not, I cannot say, but they certainly got skeptical students thinking about Christianity in a positive and intellectually honest fashion.

DECONSTRUCTING JESUS

As stated earlier, I don't believe the Church should fear postmodernism as a phenomenon or deconstruction as a process. After all, it was the Apostle Paul who himself acknowledged that, 'now we see only a reflection as in a mirror; then we shall see face to face. Now I know in part; then I shall know fully, even as I am fully known' (1 Corinthians 13:12). The fact is many non-believers (or people whom they know and love) have had unpleasant experiences with the Church. The Church is not perfect. It is comprised of fallible human beings who sometimes corrupt the message either by word or deed. One of the benefits a chaplain has over someone working in a parish environment is the lack of church baggage (i.e. negative associations). This presents us with an excellent opportunity to present the Gospel unencumbered by doctrine (good or bad), dogma, ritual, tradition or any other well-intentioned impediment. Not that there isn't a place for good doctrine, dogma, ritual, tradition, and the like - they all serve a useful purpose - but in a postmodern, anti-Christian environment the most powerful weapon a minister has is the irresistibility of the Gospel itself (see 1Corinthians 1:23-25).

To that end, in my capacity as a Tutor in Theology, Church History and Philosophy of Religion, I offered a course entitled: *The Words and Wisdom of Jesus*. The actual concept behind the course was very simple; it examined various aspects of Christian belief (such as sin, redemption, heaven, hell, love, marriage, etc.) and viewed them through the lens of Jesus' own words in the Bible. It was a fascinating deconstruction of Christianity and served to affirm the most basic tenets of the faith. During the course of the term we combined lectures with class discussions in an attempt to strip away centuries of cultural bias and focused instead on the clear, unadulterated words of Jesus himself. It was a very popular class and one that allowed the Gospel to stand on its own merits without ever having to 'preach' a word.

THE WORD BECAME FLESH AND DWELT AMONG US

One of the most common questions asked of chaplains who serve in university settings is: 'What is it about Christianity that is truly unique?'—after all, all religions make truth claims. This of course is an accurate statement, all religions do make truth claims and there is a kernel of truth to be found in most religious systems. However, Christianity has one aspect to it that no other system possesses—it has Jesus, the 'Word made flesh' (John 1:14).

It is virtually inevitable, that if a person takes the time to deconstruct their own existence, they are apt to arrive at the very same realization as Rene Descartes; namely that they are 'real'; that they are 'beings'; and yet they find themselves estranged from what Paul Tillich (1952) aptly called the very 'ground of being' (God). If completely honest with themselves, they will also come to realize that they are estranged in many ways from their fellow human beings. The question then logically becomes, how can they (as human beings) possibly reconnect with both the 'ground of being' (God) and with their fellow human beings, in a meaningful way? The Gospels of course, tell us that there is only one way and that is through the intercession of the one and only 'unique being', the God-Man Jesus Christ (John 14:6).

The incarnation is absolutely key to reaching a post-humanist / post-existentialist generation, because at some point their escapism will fail them and they will have to face the reality of their own pain, their own fear and their own mortality. It is against this backdrop that Christianity offers a God that is not far off, that is not abstract, that is not virtual; but a God who is real, one who weeps (as they do), one who suffers (as they do), one who has faced death (as they will) and who has triumphed over them. This is a God who can break through the wall of fantasy and escapism from the inside out and invite them into the real world of everlasting life.

CONTEMPLATIVE WORSHIP

As noted earlier, a chaplaincy shouldn't be a substitute for the local church but a compliment to it. The local church is the proper place for regular worship. However, wherever a Christian community exists it is appropriate for that community to worship the Lord together, including the celebration of the Lord's Supper. In order to avoid competing with the regular worship of local churches and to help break Generation Y's addiction to constant external stimulation, I see the quiet, reflective nature of Taizé worship as a useful tool in establishing a pattern of contemplative worship.

Taizé worship is very practical in that it can be done in small groups as well as large and it can take place virtually anywhere (provided the place is quiet). It doesn't require leadership *per se* (all are participants). It is neither pedagogical, nor is it liturgical. It is God-focused and built on prayer, the Word, contemplation and song. If it can be summed up in one expression it would be: 'be still and know that I am God' (Psalm 46:10). It is an antidote to the God-less, meaningless and ever constant din of the technological age and offers a welcome alternative to other distractions on offer to young people, their families and their friends.

DISCIPLESHIP AND TRUE HAPPINESS

As mentioned above, Generation Y would appear to seek happiness above all other things. However, their understanding of happiness is generally confused with pleasure. It is essentially a state of mind based upon one's external circumstances. Jesus however, teaches something quite different in the Beatitudes (Matthew 5). Here Jesus exhorts his followers to be happy in spite of their external circumstances, in spite of how they feel (i.e. sad, down-trodden, persecuted, etc.). Jesus teaches that happiness is a *state of being*—a state of oneness with God. He makes this clear in Matthew 6:33 and if there is a motto for ministry to postmodern, post-humanist, post-existentialist international graduate students this would be it: ' . . . seek ye first the kingdom of God and his righteousness' (Matthew 6:33). Only then can one be truly happy and life finally have real meaning. This is what I, and my fellow workers, sought not only to teach but also demonstrate to students every day, in order to play our small part in the Great Commission (Matthew 28:19).

The students served by the ministries described above are slightly more mature (though only just) than their undergraduate counterparts. Most are un-married and living abroad for the first time in their lives. They are under enormous pressure academically and they are at a crossroads where they must make important decisions about how they will spend the rest of their lives. They are also at a point where perhaps for the first time they are beginning to take seriously, life's big picture issues. Some come from Christian backgrounds and some don't. Some are secure in their faith, many (if not most) are very unsure of their faith. Some are skeptical, some cynical, and few have any concept of what it means to actually be a Christian or to live Christianly. The environment in which they find themselves is not merely indifferent to Christianity it is openly hostile towards it. It is against this backdrop that I, and others, sought to help make Disciples of Jesus Christ. Based upon my research and several years of working through the process, I have found the model below to be quite helpful.

A HOME AWAY FROM HOME

In addition to the inherent intellectual stimulation of life at university, the overall experience itself is often one of the most exciting times of a young person's life. It is often the first time they will have been on their own without the constant supervision of others (usually parents). It is a time of freedom, inquiry, exploration, and experimentation—a rite of passage from adolescence to adulthood. However, it can also be a very lonely time, especially for international students who must not only deal with the normal adjustments to campus life but to the culture shock of life in a new country.

While telecommunications, email, social networks, and the like make home seem less far away, students must still orient themselves to their new surroundings, making orientation week an excellent time for chaplains and local churches to reach out to both incoming and returning students. Over the years I have learned that the following are important:

1. Involve the local church.—This is important for several reasons. Firstly, a university chaplaincy should never be seen as a substitute for the local church. Instead it should be seen as an extension of and a feeder into the local church. Secondly, local churches have resources that a chaplain could only

dream of. Thirdly, there is power in numbers and the prayer support alone is invaluable to university chaplains.

2. Go to where the students are and don't wait until they come to you.—Students are inundated with invitations to events and their diaries fill up quickly. Simply putting up a shingle and letting people know you are there just won't work (except perhaps in a time of crisis). It is far more effective to attend events or go places where students congregate and get to know them personally. Soon, it is the chaplain who is the one being invited to student events—then one knows they are making progress.

3. Be a friend first, mentor next and pastor last.—As the research has suggested, young people (especially very bright and more mature young people) take the opinion of their friends very seriously—effective chaplains befriend students. Genuine friendship also builds trust and is the first step to becoming a mentor. Mentoring is key and more will be said about mentoring in a later chapter, but its safe to say that young people are always looking for help in dealing with the real world (that is to say, the world beyond the cloistered existence of the academy, or their computer screens). By mentoring a student, a person becomes more than just a friend they become a source of wisdom and advice as well. Lastly, be a pastor. By being a friend and mentor first the pastoral care a person provides later carries not only the authority of the Church but also the intimacy of a trusted Christian brother or sister.

4. The way to a student's heart is through his/her stomach.—As trite as it may sound, students are always looking for a hot meal. More importantly however, they seek the community of a shared meal.

5. An open hearth and an open home go a long way.—Universities are institutions and by definition they are impersonal. Students not only need but they crave hospitality and those chaplains willing to open up their homes to students will find

that they have gone a long way to developing meaningful relationships with those students.

6. Be open, honest, and vulnerable.—This is a very difficult thing for ministers to be. I remember well, being taught at seminary that in a parish setting it is often undesirable for a pastor to be too vulnerable. But in a chaplaincy setting there is much more room for self-deprecation. It is expected that chaplains will wrestle with difficult questions and share painful experiences with students. It is one of the ways a person creates empathy with them in their own journeys of faith and it is one of the ways the Church becomes authentic to them.

7. Establish healthy boundaries.—Despite the need to be open and honest and the desire to be hospitable, a chaplain (much like a parent) must still set healthy boundaries. This would include discernment about which student activities are or aren't appropriate for the chaplain to attend (such as a bachelor party, an invitation to which I recently respectfully declined); and what areas of student life are no-go areas (such as difficulties with academic supervisors which must remain the purview of the university's administration).

INTERCESSORY PRAYER

Throughout my time as a pastor and a chaplain, I have found one resource to be superior to all others, and that is prayer. Prayer takes many forms and often happens spontaneously, however, I would recommend that people seeking to reach Generation Y remember that they are in a spiritual battle and that they set aside specific times for specific prayer needs, including the needs of your ministry; its leaders; the university or institution where you serve; the city or town in which you live; the Church; the students themselves and their families. If I have learned anything in my time as a chaplain, it's that I can never pray too much, too often or for too many. God is a very good listener.

While the ideas expressed above represent the foundation principles upon which the Oxford Pastorate, the Graduate Christian Union and the Oxford American Mission were built, they are applicable to parish ministries as well and to support that theory, I would like to turn our attention to what I call the 'three pillars' of ministry to Generation Y: pastoral care and counseling, Christian apologetics, and Christian mentoring.

4

Pastoral Care and Counseling in Theory and Praxis

THEOLOGICAL TRADITIONS

Christian counseling is never done in a theological vacuum. Every counselor brings with him/herself a certain theological pre-disposition. In my case that pre-disposition is an amalgamation of several theological traditions from Roman Catholicism to Reformed Evangelicalism.

In the Roman Catholic tradition, Christian counseling *per se* is virtually non-existent. If a person has something of a personal nature to discuss with a priest, that conversation is most likely to take place within the confines of the confessional. This is due largely to the Roman Catholic Church's traditional theology of absolution as the primary means of overcoming one's difficulties. This was brought home to me on a personal level when seeking the counsel of a parish priest as a young adult. Struggling with fundamental questions of authority and doctrine, I visited a parish priest (in the confessional) with the intent of working through difficult theological issues with the assistance of a religious professional.

Instead of a pastoral experience however, I was roundly berated for questioning the authority of the Church and was implored to confess my theological impertinence. Needless to say this did not have the desired affect and the event was a major contributor in my eventual decision to leave the Roman Catholic Church.

Eventually I became a member of (and an ordained minister in) the Reformed Church in America whose theology is deeply rooted in sixteenth-century Calvinism and whose approach to Christian counseling is decidedly mixed. On the one hand there is a clear bias toward the responsibility of individuals to own up to their own sinfulness and to conform to the will of God as expressed in the Bible. This approach is sometimes referred to as "nouthetic" counseling and may be reviewed rather exhaustively in the work of Dr. Jay Adams (1970). However, this is not the only approach prevalent in the Reformed Church in America. The Reformed Church in America in both the eastern part of the United States and the far west, has embraced a more secular approach to counseling; and it is not uncommon to witness practitioners adapting secular practices for use in specifically Christian settings. This approach is well attested to in the works of Lawrence Crabb (1977) and Howard Clinebell (1984) and is widely accepted in both parish settings and church-associated Christian counseling centres. There has also been a movement since the middle of the twentieth-century to adapt the 'positive-thinking' theology of Norman Vincent Peale (himself an R.C.A. pastor) into various counseling settings (although in many circles this approach is considered passé).

However, in the mid-western section of the United States and in the more conservative congregations both in the east and the far west the most common approach to Christian counseling has been to combine the basic tenets of both the nouthetic and the secular / psychoanalytical approaches in a fashion similar to that described by the likes of Gary Collins (1988) and H. Newton Maloney (2007). It is this integrated approach that I have found to be most helpful when seeking to provide Christian counseling in contexts as varied as suburban evangelical congregations (whether in America or England) and as a chaplain serving a secular university.

In the case of a chaplaincy, the role of a Christian counselor is rather different from that of a parish-based counselor; and one area that is significantly different is one's attention to theological tradition. Regardless of one's own theological tradition, when a pastor is serving a parish, he or she must be particularly mindful of, and be faithful to, the traditions of the congregation served. Chaplains however are in a very different situation. Chaplains are by definition religious professionals that serve in an otherwise secular setting. This requires them to be aware of, and sensitive to, a wide variety of theological traditions. Chaplains also need to be mindful of the fact that they will often encounter people who have no theological background or religious frame of reference at all. This is especially true in a university setting where people are drawn from a wide spectrum of the population where theological ignorance and biblical illiteracy are often the norm.

Due to the inquisitive nature of the academic experience however, many students are often at least interested in developing an understanding of theology and all things spiritual and will sometimes engage the services of a chaplain for just that purpose. Unfortunately, university chaplaincies tend not to be proactive in reaching out to students, and prefer instead to wait until students seek them out, before engaging in conversations about God and faith.

As I discovered during previous research into this topic however, this may not be the most effective model for a chaplain to employ. In a previous academic tome I contend that: 'the Church has a responsibility to "go" wherever there are hurting people and not merely be content to "hang its shingle" on the side of a building and say "come inside" if you think you might need us'.[1]

In my experience some graduate students seem to sense their own spiritual inadequacies and are quite comfortable seeking out the counsel of a chaplain. Others however are not and they need to be given opportunities to reflect on theological and spiritual

---

1. Kenneth J. Barnes, *The Deployment of Dual Career Ministers as Corporate Chaplains in a Post-industrial Society* (MPhil Thesis: University of London), 2002, p. 77.

matters generally, before addressing their own spiritual needs specifically. As mentioned previously, in the case of my own ministry at Oxford University, opportunities for this sort of reflection were made available to students in various forms, including lectures, round-table discussions and various forums. These diverse settings provided an opportunity for students from all theological backgrounds, or no theological background, to engage with religious professionals and fellow students in order to work through any number of spiritual issues. Furthermore, the opportunity to make contact and develop relationships with students, within the context of theological discourse, renders 'one on one' sessions with a chaplain less daunting for students in need of pastoral care.

DEMOGRAPHICS

In theory, a chaplaincy to graduate students could involve people from any number of age groups and there are indeed many mature students studying at Oxford University. However, the most common age group represented may best be described as 'single young adults' and / or Generation Y. These students experience many of the same issues that people in this age group experience in a parish setting (i.e. issues surrounding life-coping skills; spiritual identity; moral crises, etc.), however, the uniqueness of a university setting exacerbates many of the problems they face and makes counseling graduate students slightly more complex.

In the first instance, graduate students at Oxford University are exceptionally bright people. They are not only naturally intelligent; they have learnt to hone both their inquisitive as well as their rhetorical skills. This makes engaging them in discussions about spiritual issues especially challenging. For example, they may not be content to merely engage in a discussion about the existence of God, they may insist instead on debating issues of epistemology first, before even considering the question of God's existence, etc.

This became evident when I first arrived in Oxford and began serving as a chaplain. The original intent was to host a weekly fellowship event, where students and I could engage with each other in a casual atmosphere. The idea was to develop personal relationships with the students first and then slowly explore theological issues together. The students however, had a very different idea. They were happy to have informal gatherings, but they wanted those gatherings to be more than just opportunities for casual fellowship. They wanted to be challenged intellectually and spiritually and they asked that our meetings become formal, and the weekly apologetics group was formed.

While I happily agreed to their request, it meant a significant change in preparation. It meant preparing to discuss a wide range of topics from philosophy to metaphysics and to engage in such discussions at a reasonably high level of competence. This is not something that most parish-based pastor / counselors are required to do. If the meetings were going to be meaningful to the students however, and if I was going to have any credibility with the students, then I would have to adjust my plans accordingly.

This is exactly what I did and the result was not only an opportunity to sharpen my own rhetorical skills, but it gave me the opportunity to meet with students in both group and private settings. This led to some very deep and meaningful relationships developing and ultimately pastoral care and counseling ensued. It also gave me an excellent forum from which to challenge the previously mentioned 'happy midi-narrative' with the Judeo-Christian meta-narrative.

Another significant difference between the demographic make-up of a typical parish and that of a university chaplaincy is the multi-national / multi-cultural nature of the student population. While my ministry was called the Oxford American Mission and was targeted toward U.S. expatriate students, in fact students from all over the world were part of the post-graduate community served by that ministry. This added yet another level of complexity that parish-based pastor / counselors may not always face. This demographic reality requires a person to be especially careful with the language he or she uses and demands a knowledge of and sensitivity to a wide variety of cultures. Fortunately, in my case, prior to becoming a university chaplain I was an international business executive who had done business on six continents and travelled extensively across Europe, Asia, the Middle East and India particularly. Many students found my familiarity with their home countries both comforting and reassuring and often proved a valuable icebreaker when first meeting foreign students.

Lastly, post-graduate students live in a unique world of heightened expectations and extreme stress. They are under a tremendous amount of pressure, both internally and externally, to perform at a very high level of academic achievement and to meet strict submission deadlines. Most post-graduates live far away from home; are working outside the normal rhythm of college life and spend most of their time doing research. In short, they tend to be lonely. This combination of factors makes it all the more important for chaplains to reach out to graduate students in order to give them the social support they need to survive the rigors of academic life.

FRAME OF REFERENCE

As with people in a local parish, there are post-graduate students whose frames of reference are influenced by any number (or combination) of world-views. They may tend toward traditionalism, modernism and/or postmodernism depending on a wide variety of influences in their lives. It seems to me however that a student's world-view is also very likely to be influenced by his or her subject area. For instance, students who work in the physical sciences often tend toward a modernist world-view. Upon reflection this makes a great deal of sense, as it was the emergence of modern science that gave birth to much of the thinking that helped form modernism as we know it today (although one stark exception appears to be the area of quantum physics, which challenges many of the most basic principles of observability and measurability so central to both modern science and modernism).

In the humanities and social sciences however, students tend to be far more influenced by postmodernism, although there are exceptions to this rule as well, especially if a student already holds strong religious convictions.

What I found to be absolutely critical however, in providing pastoral care and counseling to post-graduate students, was my ability and willingness to work with students dialogically as opposed to pedagogically. This is probably due to the collegiate nature of the academy, the maturity of the students, the lack of common theological background among the students, the secular nature of the setting and the intellectual intensity of the environment. That is not to suggest that post-graduate students are incapable of, or unwilling to receive clear guidance from a religious professional. It simply suggests that the method with which a person communicates that guidance needs to reflect a community of peers.

Furthermore, in a chaplaincy setting, one may find that students are less likely to concern themselves with specific doctrines than they are with universal truths. That said they do expect a chaplain to be thoroughly honest about his or her own religious beliefs and to be consistent in how he or she defends those beliefs. In my case, my Calvinist leanings were no secret, however it wasn't my role to champion one particular tradition over another unless the tenets of that tradition proved particularly useful in an apologetic setting.

Being open and honest about one's own theological convictions further adds to a chaplain's credibility with his or her students. While many graduate students enjoy theological debate and the cut and thrust of philosophical discourse, they none the less expect a chaplain to know what he or she believes to be true. Some students may not agree with a chaplain's theology, but they still expect the chaplain to have carefully and faithfully thought-out his or her beliefs before entrusting them with their own spiritual journey. To use an analogy, they may or may not be interested in where their guide has been, but they certainly expect him or her to be competent with a map and compass.

Students also have an expectation of professionalism and competence; knowledge of the academy and its unique demands; spiritual as well as intellectual integrity and of course, strict confidentiality. This is not to suggest that a university chaplain needs to be a genius (or even a scholar for that matter), but one should be both willing and able to engage students on an intellectual level. This may require a chaplain to prepare for topics that are not his or her own greatest strength; but even a cursory understanding of a student's topic can go a long way in establishing both empathy and trust (key ingredients in any pastoral / counseling relationship). That is not to say that chaplains must master every academic subject, but they would do well to do as the Apostle Paul suggests: 'be all things to all men . . . in order to save them' (2 Corinthians 9:22); and as with any counseling situation, students want to know that their personal situation will not end up as a Sunday sermon illustration. Similarly, I have gone to great lengths to ensure that the case studies below are sufficiently opaque so as not to be easily recognizable.

SPIRITUAL CRISIS—A TRUE STORY

Paula was a DPhil candidate in Philosophy of Religion, however she also had a great deal of experience and knowledge in the physical sciences, and at one time considered a career in physics. Her research into other religions and faith traditions had caused her to question the basic tenets of her own Christian faith. This of course is not an uncommon phenomenon for philosophy students. She was also very interested in the recent works of Professor Richard Dawkins, especially *The God Delusion* that was published during her tenure at Oxford University. She knew that she was having a crisis of faith but she wasn't comfortable speaking to anyone directly about her situation. Instead she continued to keep her own counsel and her doubts started to take their toll on her walk with the Lord. She found it hard to go to church and to pray and was uncomfortable with the way many prominent Christians framed their theological arguments. She was having a genuine spiritual crisis.

As an American student she became involved with the Oxford American Mission and soon she and her husband developed a pastoral as well as a personal (quasi-parental) relationship with my wife and I. Soon she felt comfortable enough with this new circle of friends to share her struggle with us as well as some of her fellow graduate students. A break-through came when she attended one of the weekly apologetics meetings. The discussion that evening was on the topic of 'irreducible complexity'. Space here does not permit a detailed explanation of the concept of irreducible complexity, but suffice to say it is one of the many scientific arguments used by Christians to prove the existence (or at least the probability) of the existence of God. In the course of the discussion it became obvious to me that she not only found the irreducibility argument unsatisfactory, she actually found all of the traditional teleological arguments wanting as well.

Later, in a one-on-one meeting with her, I decided to take a different tack and appealed instead to her obvious interest in philosophy. Instead of focusing on the teleological arguments, I encouraged her to consider the ontological case for the existence of God; not the classic formulation of St. Anselm, mind you, but a more basic (and far more satisfying) argument from 'being' itself as expressed by the likes of Descartes, Kierkegaard, Tillich and others. This approach ultimately had the desired effect as evidenced by her proclamation at a subsequent apologetics meeting that for her the uniqueness (and appeal) of Christianity was simply this: ' . . . and the Word became flesh and dwelt among us' (John 1:14) and no additional proofs (for her at least) of the existence of God were necessary.

It was a 'road to Damascus' experience for Paula and a revelation for me as well. The counseling that transpired was a direct result of me gaining the student's trust and respect as well as providing settings that encouraged theological and spiritual discourse. It also demonstrated the fact that Christianity has weapons at its disposal that are well suited to the onslaught of both postmodernism and New Atheism.

ACADEMIC CRISIS—A TRUE STORY

Ram was an MPhil / DPhil student studying economics. Before progressing to DPhil candidacy, MPhil students must first demonstrate their academic competency to their supervisors. This is often a formality as students accepted into graduate programs at Oxford University are already proven to be capable scholars. However, there are occasions when things go badly, especially it would seem, for international students.

The reasons why international students seem to encounter more difficulties in this area than their British counterparts is open to debate. There has been speculation in the British press recently that universities are so motivated by the financial benefits of admitting overseas students (who pay much higher tuition fees than home students) that they create in an influx of less capable scholars that must ultimately be weeded out by faculties. There is no hard evidence to support this hypothesis of course, but it is not beyond the realm of possibility. It also may be that the educational systems from whence international students come are so drastically different from the British system that expectations are easily misunderstood. Perhaps some supervisors are bullies; or perhaps, as appeared to be the case for Ram, some international students are simply the victims of long-held prejudices.

Bullying and prejudice of course are not uniquely British phenomena, but they do seem rampant at institutions that have a long association with the British Establishment. Whatever the cause however, the results of an unsatisfactory relationship between a student and his or her supervisor can be devastating for the student, often destroying their confidence and sometimes ending their fledgling careers.

Ram was an active member of the Graduate Christian Union and known to me through my GCU contacts and activities. Although he was not an American student he was none the less involved in several Oxford American Mission events, including some of the social events, such as the annual Thanksgiving dinner (a very popular event with international students). Ram is an extremely confident, articulate and gregarious person who is unabashed about his Christian faith. However, as a young man of colour, from a developing nation with an outspoken belief in God, he was in a distinct minority among his fellow scholars and according to Ram was barely tolerated by his own supervisor.

While his supervisor seemed to work well with him at first (at least on a professional level), the nearer the time came for him to be approved for advancement from MPhil status to DPhil status, the more strained the relationship became. Finally, things came to a head when he was berated by his supervisor for including a quotation from the Bible in one of his papers, which the supervisor found to be both gratuitous and juvenile. In the course of their discussions over the matter the supervisor let slip that she could not understand why students from the Indian Sub-continent were even admitted to the University as their educational experiences and intellectual abilities were clearly not up to Oxford's high standards[2].

Needless to say, Ram was completely shattered by his experience. Not only had he been taken to task for quoting the Bible, he had been accused of intellectual inferiority on the basis of his nationality (read ethnicity). It was nothing less than soul destroying and he sought my pastoral care and counsel.

Why Ram chose to seek the counsel of a chaplain when he knew and had access to other religious professionals was based on several factors:

1. He knew that I had once been an international graduate student at a British university and assumed (correctly) that I would be sympathetic to his experience.

2. He hoped that I might be able to give him some practical advice on how to lodge a formal appeal should such an appeal be necessary.

2. It is important to note that the circumstances described only reflect the recollection and perceived experience of the student. I am not making any accusations about the supervisor in question or the University. However, in a pastoral / counseling setting one must deal with the experience of the subject by starting with the problem as perceived by the subject himself.

3. He was comfortable with me on a personal level—as with Paula, my wife and I had become parent figures to him.

4. He knew if nothing else that I would pray for him.

Over the ensuing months, Ram met with me on numerous occasions to discuss his plight and to pray. I needed to make clear to him however, that while I did indeed empathise with him and would give him as much advice as possible, I could not actually intervene in any way with the University or his department; that would be the responsibility of the departmental chair and / or other university officials. While I did encourage him to defend himself against what seemed to be a blatant case of prejudice and to exhaust whatever appeal procedures were available to him, I also warned him that the probability of success was very low. The academic community is quite adept at defending their own and when that community is also associated with the British Establishment it is very nearly an immovable object.

Instead, I concentrated on helping him come to terms with his situation in spite of the injustice of it all. I encouraged him to have faith in the sovereignty of God and know that in the person of the persecuted Christ, God stood in solidarity with his suffering. I encouraged him to find forgiveness for the person who brought this calamity upon him; and mostly, I encouraged him not to lose hope. In short, I encouraged him to be happy in the way that Jesus had taught his disciples to be happy in the Beatitudes (i.e. to be happy in spite of persecution) and I encouraged him to rely solely on the one friend who would not let him down in his time of need—the Lord Jesus Christ.

Ram is an immensely intelligent and capable person and despite this setback I also encouraged him to remain committed to the calling he had received from God to pursue an academic career. Even after his appeal was rejected and he left the University without his doctorate, Ram and I remained in contact through the Internet. Over the ensuing months I continued to support him in prayer and encouraged him to keep pushing on doors until the right one opened up; reminding him that if it was indeed God's will that he should return to Oxford, God would make it happen. Then, one day I received an email from Ram asking whether I would be willing to provide a reference for him. He had applied for a new degree at Oxford University in a different (but related department) and was confident that God was indeed calling him back to the U.K. Now of course, I could officially intervene and I provided both a written and a verbal reference on his behalf. Happily, he was accepted and returned once again to Oxford University to pursue his studies. He also returned a stronger, wiser and more determined individual—pursuing his dream and following God's call into the academy. It was an extremely difficult and trying experience but one that fortunately had a happy ending. As the next story will demonstrate however, that isn't always the case.

PERSONAL CRISIS—A TRUE STORY

Sam was a mature student doing a DPhil at the Saïd Business School of Oxford University. It is not uncommon for mature students to attend business school. In fact, most students who attend are career executives from multi-national companies seeking to enhance their careers by earning advanced professional degrees (typically an MBA). Sam's case however was rather different. Sam had already been a successful senior executive but his career and his life were left in ruins when he became involved in a high profile business failure. He not only lost his job and his fortune, he lost his wife, his family and his sense of purpose in life. Sam had come to Oxford to start over. Sadly, things did not go very smoothly.

As with many unmarried students, Sam lived in shared accommodation, a kind of boarding house, run by a local charity. He was not himself a practicing Christian but he did show an interest in Christianity and had grown up in a Methodist household. He occasionally attended church services and even one or two events sponsored by the Graduate Christian Union and it was at one such event that Sam and I met. During our brief exchange I gave him a business card with the contact details of the Oxford American Mission but our paths never crossed again—until he was in crisis.

As with many research students, Sam's existence was a very lonely one and as with everyone associated with the Saïd Business School his academic workload was extremely demanding. It also became obvious to me (later on) that Sam had never properly dealt with his immense loss or processed the magnitude of his grief. Instead, he pressed ahead with his studies and soon the pressures of academic life, coupled with his loneliness and unprocessed grief, were too much for him to bear and instead of seeking help, he began to self-medicate by indulging in excessive amounts of alcohol.

Alcohol and drug abuse are rampant at universities across the world. Often these things are abused strictly for recreational purposes. Sometimes however (as in Sam's case) they are a desperate cry for help. Fortunately for Sam the house in which he lived was run by a group of nuns who genuinely cared for their tenants and who saw themselves as a pastors as well as landlords. One day, one of the sisters found Sam passed out in a drunken stupor and as she was cleaning up his mess, she saw my business card lying on top of a dresser. She called me on the telephone and together we began to seek ways in which to help a very desperate student.

Upon seeing Sam and learning about his condition from Sister Michael Anne, I knew that I was dealing with a substance abuse issue that I was ill prepared to treat. I also sensed that there might be other clinical or even pathological issues that required medical attention. Thus began a team effort to get Sam the professional help he needed. It would prove to be a very difficult task.

First we engaged the help of a local physician. Unfortunately, there was little he could do other than to provide moral support (and also ensure that the drinking hadn't yet caused any obvious physical damage). So it was decided that the best course of action would be to have Sam admitted (reluctantly, but with his consent) to a substance abuse treatment centre.

Fortunately, I had contacts at a centre run by another Christian charity. However, the rules of the centre are quite strict and they insist that the person being admitted is not intoxicated at the time of admission. By the time Sam and I had left the doctor's office that afternoon, I thought he was sober enough for admittance later that day. Naively, I dropped Sam off at the boarding house and instructed him to pack a bag for an extended stay at the centre. I then went home briefly and sorted my affairs so that I would be free for the 120-mile round-trip drive to the centre. An hour later when I returned to the boarding house, I found that Sam had not only failed to pack a bag, he had somehow sourced and consumed a huge amount of alcohol and had once again passed out drunk in his room. Instead of going to the treatment centre, we went to the emergency room of the local hospital.

Hospital emergency rooms are very busy places and they don't like using up beds for people who have voluntarily incapacitated themselves with alcohol. They would only allow Sam to remain in the hospital until they were sure he was not in imminent danger from alcohol poisoning. Within two hours of arriving he was discharged from the hospital. During that time, I made a desperate plea to the centre to allow Sam to be admitted despite his current state of drunkenness. The centre reluctantly agreed and that evening we drove to the centre in order for him to begin his much needed and long overdue in-house treatment for alcohol addiction.

The next day however, I realised that Sam had never actually packed a bag of clothes for his stay at the centre, so I took one of my own suitcases to a nearby department store and filled it with clothes for him to wear during his convalescence. Unfortunately, when I arrived at the centre an hour later, I was informed that Sam had already checked himself out and that he had taken a train back to Oxford. Within minutes of arriving back in Oxford he proceeded to find alcohol and get drunk all over again.

To say that it was a frustrating experience would be an understatement; it was devastating and both Sister Michael Anne and I felt totally helpless. This kind of activity (getting drunk, going to the hospital, pledging sobriety, getting drunk again, etc.) would go on for months until one Sunday there appeared to be a genuine breakthrough. At a worship service held at a nearby church, Sam purportedly made the decision to give his life to Christ and become a practicing Christian. For a while, he did indeed stay sober, but sadly he soon returned to his old habits and his condition once again deteriorated. I am afraid I don't have a happy ending to report. In fact, I have lost track of Sam and the last report I received wasn't very encouraging. None the less I do have hope that he will (with God's help) overcome his afflictions and get back onto a path to wellbeing, but it will undoubtedly require both medical as well as pastoral intervention and for that to happen Sam must himself decide that he wants the cycle of misery to end.

Providing pastoral care and counseling is always a daunting task; but with the support of other like-minded servants of Christ and by the grace of God, progress can be made and healing can be found. Sister Michael Anne is a saint in my book and an inspiration to anyone seeking the cure of souls, but we can both attest to the fact that there are no guarantees in terms of success. Despite the well-intentioned efforts of religious and other professionals, some people simply don't get better; but that shouldn't discourage us from doing our best to help them. After all, as a very wise pastor once taught me at the very start of my ministry, 'God doesn't call us to be "successful", he calls us to be "obedient" and we have to leave the results of our efforts to him and his divine grace.' They are words that I have never forgotten and for which I am eternally grateful.

5

Christian Apologetics from a Reformed Perspective

As mentioned in the previous chapter, pastoral care and counseling never happens in a theological vacuum. The same can be said of apologetics. If I learned anything in my time as a chaplain to Generation Y it's the importance of sound apologetics supported by good theology. In my case that means Reformed theology (including covenant theology in particular). Whether one agrees with my theology or not, I hope the following pages will demonstrate at least two things: 1.) that the arguments posed by the New Atheists are not unassailable; and 2.) good theological constructs are key to refuting the claims of Christianity's opponents.

I know that not every believer subscribes to the importance of Christian apologetics. Some would simply prefer to quote pertinent passages from the Bible and let it go at that. However, merely appealing to passages of Scripture won't mean much if our listeners don't recognize the authority of the Bible to begin with. Likewise, we must understand an opponent's position before attempting a logical rebuttal to that position, which is why honing our apologetic skills is very important, especially when seeking to reach a generation as skeptical (and critical) as Generation Y. Interestingly enough, despite the sensations stirred up in the media over such issues as sexual ethics, gender and other contentious points of doctrine, these things tend not to be the key stumbling blocks when attempting to reach Generation Y with the Gospel. It's actually the big picture issues they struggle with, such as the existence of God and the problem of evil; topics that are often overlooked or given little consideration at theological college / seminary.

As noted previously, the *Oxford Dictionary of the Christian Church* defines apologetics as, 'the defense of the Christian faith on intellectual grounds by trained theologians and philosophers'. While I wouldn't expect everyone reading this book to become a theologian or a philosopher *per se*, I believe that everyone in ministry needs to at least acquaint themselves with apologetics as a discipline and with the issues that mean the most to Generation Y. While serving in the academy where there is open hostility toward Christianity and where relativism and postmodernity reign supreme, I have found apologetics particularly useful, and while that has been normative at universities for a very long time, it is becoming more common in our towns, cities and local parishes as well.

Largely due to the challenges discussed above apologetics has become a popular topic in recent years, especially in evangelical circles; however, the Church has a long and varied tradition of making a rational defense of its truth claims, beginning with the example of Jesus himself. As James Sire states in his book, *Habits of the Mind* (2000):

> as the Logos, Jesus Christ is the epistemological foundation for our ability to reason. He is Jesus the Reasoner. As the incarnate Son of God, Jesus Christ is the prime example of how we should think.[1]

He points out that Jesus often employed various methods of argument and persuasion to make his points, such as simple analogies and *a fortiori* arguments.

---

1. James W. Sire, *Habits of the Mind* (Dower's Grove: Intervarsity Press, 2000), p. 184.

To illustrate this, Sire points to Jesus' defense of his actions on the Sabbath in the Fourth Gospel. In this passage, Jesus defends the fact that he has healed a man on the Sabbath day. However, he not only defends his actions, he reveals the source of his authority to act in this way and does so by employing *a fortiori* arguments. Analogizing his healing of a man on the Sabbath with the Jewish custom of circumcising on the Sabbath, Jesus says:

> I did one deed and you all marvel. On this account Moses has given you circumcision (not because it is from Moses, but because it is from the fathers), and on the Sabbath you circumcise a man. If a man receives circumcision on the Sabbath that the Law of Moses may not be broken, are you angry with me because I made an entire man well on the Sabbath (John 7:21b-23)?

The argument is perfectly logical. If it is lawful to perform a limited act of healing on the Sabbath (circumcision), in order to honor the divine decree (the Law), then surely it is even more appropriate to perform a complete act of healing in order to honor God himself.

Furthermore, Sire notes that Jesus was not averse to using reason and sustained intellectual arguments to support his claims. As Sire puts it:

> One way we reason is to give 'reasons' why we take something to be true. That is, we make a case for our views. This is precisely what Jesus does in the fifth chapter of John.[2]

Once again, defending his actions on the Sabbath, Jesus states:

> . . . truly, truly I say unto you, the Son can do nothing of Himself, unless it is something He sees the Father doing; for whatever the Father does, these things the Son also does in like manner. For the Father loves the Son, and shows Him all things that He Himself is doing; and greater works than these will He show Him, that you may marvel (John 5:19b-20).

2. Sire, *Habits of the Mind*, p. 191.

In Jesus' 'epistemology', doing God's will is integrally connected with 'knowing' (coming to understand with confidence) whether Jesus' teaching is from God . . . except a brief aside (see John 7:53-8:11), John 7-8 constitutes one sustained argument.[3]

The Apostle Paul of course also employed the disciplines we associate with apologetics while on his missionary journeys, whether engaging with fellow Jews in the synagogue or Gentiles in the marketplace and various centers of learning. As we shall examine in more detail below, his encounter with the Athenians at the Areopagus (Acts 17) is, as Professor McGrath puts it, 'an object lesson in apologetics', but it is not the only example available to us.

Throughout his ministry, Paul consistently argued for the reasonableness and the logic of his beliefs. Whether using analogies to Old Testament figures such as Abraham, or Moses or Adam; or simply declaring the 'wisdom which God predestined before the ages' (1 Corinthians 2:6b), Paul stated clearly if not always succinctly, the sublime truth of the Christian faith.

Additionally, the Apostle Peter clearly instructs the early church to, 'always be ready to make a defense to everyone who asks you to give an account for the hope that is in you, yet with gentleness and reverence' (1 Peter 3: 15b).

This was an instruction that the early church took very seriously, that resulted in an apologetic tradition that has lasted to the present day.

Among the first of the better-known early apologists, were Justin Martyr (c.100 AD—c.165 AD) and Quintus Septimius Florens Tertullian (c.160 AD—c.225 AD). They demonstrated, not only the early church's commitment to apologetics, but also two distinct approaches to apologetics, the remnants of which still exist today.

The first approach, employed by Justin Martyr is sometimes referred to as the 'positive' or 'liberal' approach. The second, employed by Tertullian is sometimes known as the 'negative' or 'rigorist' approach; and in many ways bears a striking resemblance

3. Sire, *Habits of the Mind*, p. 193.

to the pre-suppositional approach of some later Reformed theologians. As Justin Martyr states in his *First Apology*:

> For, myself, when I learned of the wicked disguise which through false report was cast over divine teaching of Christians by evil demons in order to turn away others, I laughed at this disguise and at the opinions of the multitude; and I declare that I prayed and strove with all my might to be found a Christian, not because the teachings of Plato are contrary to those of Christ, but because they are not in all respects like them; and as is the case of the doctrines of the others, Stoics, poets and prose-authors. For each discoursed rightly, seeing that which was kin to Christianity through a share in the seminal divine reason (*logos*); but they that have uttered contrary opinions seem not to have had the invisible knowledge and irrefutable wisdom. Whatever has been uttered aright by any men in any place belongs to us Christians; for, next to God, we worship and love reason (*logos*) which is from the unbegotten and ineffable God ... For all authors were able to see the truth darkly, through the implanted seed of reason (*logos*) dwelling in them. For the seed and imitation of a thing, given according to a man's capacity, is one thing; far different is the thing itself, the sharing of which and its representation is given according to his grace (*Apology* II.x.iii).

In this paragraph, Justin Martyr establishes several principles of the positive view of apologetics. In the first instance, he implicitly acknowledges that while there is a neutral marketplace of ideas where the truth claims of Christianity will be compared to other religions and philosophies, there is also a spiritual battle taking place, where evil demons seek to turn people away from the Gospel message. In response to that realization, he laughs (apparently at the futility of the enemy to hold any sway over the will of God); prays (ostensibly for the strength and wisdom to counteract the enemy's efforts); and strives to be 'found a Christian'; that is to say, to hold fast to the Gospel.

That said however, he still acknowledges the fact that other philosophies and writings do express certain truths. Unfortunately, they do not represent the whole truth. They are filled with error and lack the 'invisible knowledge and the irrefutable wisdom' that can only come from God. Echoing the words of the Apostle Paul in 1 Corinthians 13, he states that purveyors of other philosophies are only able to 'see the truth darkly'; yet that veiled and imperfect truth still has some value as emanating from the 'unbegotten and ineffable God'; and as such even 'belongs to us Christians'.

This approach however, is strikingly different from the apologetic thinking of Tertullian who states that:

> . . . heresies themselves are prompted by philosophy. Heretics and philosophers handle the same subject matter; both treat of the same topics—Whence came evil? And why? Whence came man? And how? And a question lately posed by Valentinus—Whence came God? . . . Wretched Aristotle! Who taught them dialect, that art of building and demolishing . . . What is there in common between Athens and Jerusalem? What between the Academy and the Church? What between heretics and Christians? . . . Away with all projects for a 'Stoic', a 'Platonist' or a 'dialectic' Christianity! After Christ Jesus we desire no subtle theories, no acute enquiries after the Gospel . . . (*Heretics* VII).

Tertullian's repudiation of non-Christian belief systems is both complete and uncompromising. His distrust of all things academic is palpable. It would appear that for Tertullian, any positive attributes that one could possibly ascribe to non-Christian philosophies are rendered irrelevant by the potential damage caused by the errant elements of those philosophies. For Tertullian, it is the Gospel or nothing and he has clearly cast his lot with the former.

A similar view of apologetics has been expressed in more recent years in the writings of Cornelius Van Til, lately Professor of Apologetics at Westminster Theological Seminary. Basing his position largely on an exegesis of 1 Corinthians 1:20-21, Van Til asks:

> What answer had Socrates, Plato and Aristotle been able to give to the deepest problems of life? Shall we say that they gave no answer? No, indeed; for they could not

escape giving an answer. But the answers they had given were wrong. Their wisdom had been made foolish with God. In the light of the narrative which Paul brought, the wisdom of the Greeks was not merely inadequate; it was sinful.[4]

This is a remarkable statement in light of Van Til's unwavering admiration for John Calvin. For Calvin himself declares in his seminal work *The Institutes of the Christian Religion*:

> I deny not, indeed, that in the writings of the philosophers we meet occasionally with shrewd and apposite remarks on the nature of God . . . the Lord has bestowed on them some slight perception of his Godhead (*Inst* 2.2.18).

Van Til however, seems to hold a dramatically different opinion. He rejects in the strongest possible terms, the Roman Catholic emphasis on the *Imago Dei*, which he sees as having no epistemological value whatsoever; and likewise rebukes the ontological case and what he calls 'analogy of being' arguments. 'The God of Aristotle', he states simply, 'is not the God of Christianity', and 'the moral of all this for Protestants should surely be to challenge the wisdom of the world in every dimension. For Van Til, the only 'point of contact' between Christians and non-Christians is that of 'head-on collision'.

As Robert Brenton rightly observes in an article written for *Apologia Magazine*:

> Van Til base(d) his apologetics in the biblical revelation of Christian theism . . . as revealed in the Scriptures of the Old and New Testaments, a body of truth—or if you will—a *system* of truth, which comes to us not in piecemeal, but as a UNIT.[5]

4. Cornelius Van Til, *The Intellectual Challenge of the Gospel* (London: Tyndale, 1950), p. 1.

5. Robert Brenton, 'The Apologetic Programme of Cornelius Van Til as an Assault Against the Apologetic Tradition,' *Apologia*, 5.2 (1996), p. 20-25.

Furthermore, he appears to reject the traditional Calvinist understanding of 'general' and 'special' revelation as being distinct, and sees them as two sides of the same coin—especially in his treatment of 'natural' revelation. Van Til states that:

> Man was never left to the study of natural revelation alone. Natural revelation was from the outset of history accompanied and supplemented by supernatural revelation. The two were involved with one another; they were supplemental to one another. They are unintelligible the one without the other. There has been no time in the history of the human race when man was expected to look at nature alone and ask whether God exists.[6]

While his zeal for the uncompromising truth of the Gospel is commendable, I can't help but wonder whether such an approach is actually helpful in seeking to promote the Gospel of Jesus Christ in the aforementioned 'marketplace of ideas'? Professor McGrath would think not. While he acknowledges the fact that Van Til has (rightly) 'shown the necessity of grounding apologetics upon a sound theological foundation', he questions whether his overall system is effective; and highlights the fact that Van Til's system represents a significant departure from the thinking of Calvin and other Reformed theologians. Indeed, Van Til's system is a departure from the traditional method of doing apologetics and his basis for making that departure is firmly rooted in his belief that all revelation is both integral and purposeful to one's epistemology. He rejects any effort to build upon non-Christian sources as both superfluous and dangerous; leading only to error and idolatry.

To a certain extent, McGrath would appear to agree with Van Til in that natural revelation alone is inadequate to the purpose of apologetics. However, citing Calvin, McGrath sees the process (potentially) as a two-step process, whereby special revelation supplements and ultimately completes that which we know via general revelation. McGrath observes that:

---

6. Brenton, 'The Apologetic Programme,' p. 20.

Van Til's point is that natural knowledge of God, which arises from human autonomy, leads to idolatry. But the sixteenth-century Reformers such as Luther and Calvin were perfectly aware of this danger. Calvin stresses that a natural knowledge of God can easily degenerate into idolatry. Such knowledge of God is inadequate; it requires supplementation with revelation. Yet rightly understood, a natural knowledge of God is a starting point—and nothing more—for the full richness of God's self-revelation. The error in question is not *making use* of natural knowledge of God, but making *improper* use of such knowledge. If a starting point (natural knowledge of God) is confused with the end point (revealed knowledge of God the redeemer), a serious distortion of the kind feared by Van Til will result. But as Calvin stresses, it need not. It is up to the apologist to uncover—that is to say, raise to explicit consciousness—and to make the best use of that 'suppressed knowledge' and allow it to lead on to greater and better things.[7]

In comparing these two positions, one may rightly ask whether Van Til's system constitutes apologetics at all, or whether he is actually espousing a kind of intellectually based kerygmatic formula. One may also rightly ask the question posed by Tertullian (above) 'does Athens have anything to do with Jerusalem?' And if so, where indeed is the point of contact?

It would seem from the biblical evidence that the Apostle Paul believed whole-heartedly that Athens has much to do with Jerusalem, or at least vice versa. One need only examine closely the experience of the Apostle himself while in Athens, as found in the seventeenth chapter of the Book of Acts (Acts 17:16-34) to come to this conclusion.

In the beginning of the narrative, we see that Paul is concerned about the idolatry he encounters in the city and 'his spirit was being provoked' (Acts 17:16) to address the issue. So he went both to the synagogue where he encountered God-fearing people (both Jew and Gentile) and to the marketplace where he would

---

7. McGrath, *Bridge Building*, p. 39.

have encountered people of every (or no particular) philosophical and/or religious persuasion.

At first, Paul seeks to reason with the people. His approach at this stage was evidently to enter into a dialogue, presumably to gain the people's trust and to establish his credentials as a person of intellect. Upon establishing his credibility, however, he then felt comfortable preaching the resurrection of Jesus Christ (Acts 17:18). This method was evidently quite effective, as the leaders of the intellectual community brought Paul to the Areopagus, which had evolved over the centuries from a court of criminal justice and council of elders to a center of intellectual inquiry. They made clear the fact that they took new ideas seriously and the narrative itself states that: 'all the Athenians and the strangers visiting there used to spend their time in nothing other than telling or hearing something new' (Acts 17:21).

Once inside the Areopagus, Paul once again chose at first to reason with the people before attempting to preach to them. He first acknowledges (and it would seem commends them) on the fact that they are a 'very religious' people and that they even worship an 'Unknown God'. He then proclaimed to them that he knew who that unknown deity is (Acts 17:22-23).

Paul then goes on to explain, 'logically' the attributes of this deity:

1. He is the 'creator' of the entire universe (Acts 17:24).

2. As such he does not 'dwell' in temples that are themselves 'made by hands' (Acts 17:24).

3. Neither is he 'served' by human hands, as he himself is 'not needing' of anything (Acts 17:25).

4. He has no needs, as he is the very giver of 'life' and 'breath' to all things (Acts 17:25).

5. And he is also the sovereign creator of 'humankind' having 'appointed' all aspects of human existence (Acts 17:26).

6. He has done this in order that human beings might 'seek' to 'find him', even though he is in fact not far from any of us (Acts 17:27).

7. In fact, we 'live', 'move' and 'are' in him and we are (as even the Greek poet Aratus acknowledges) his 'children' (Acts 17:28).

8. As such, we should not think of God in material terms as though he were an 'image' formed by the 'art' or 'imagination' of human beings (Acts 17:29).

Having then established the logic of his argument, Paul moves from the apologetic to the kerygmatic as he preaches that all must repent (Acts 17:30); because God has set the day when he will judge the world. God has sent proof of his intentions having raised Jesus from the dead (Acts 17:31).

The efficacy of Paul's combination of apologetic and kerygmatic methods is made clear by the fact that while some in the crowd rejected the Gospel message, others (including the Areopagite, Dionysius) responded favorably and became believers.

As McGrath notes: 'The Areopagus sermon . . . illustrates the New Testament tendency to mingle *kerygma* and *apologia,* as the two aspects of a greater whole'[8]. I contend however, that regardless of whether one is a traditional liberal / positive apologist or a rigorist / presuppositional apologist; one theological principle that would seem to be at the very heart of the apologetic enterprise is the Reformed principle known as the *sensus divinitatis* (sense of the divine).

SENSUS DIVINITATIS AND NEW ATHEISM

Strictly speaking, the Bible does not explicitly state that a *sensus divinitatis* exists, however it is a theology that is based upon both biblical evidence (i.e. Psalm 10:11; Psalm 14:1; Psalm 36:1; Acts 17:16-34; Romans 1:19-21; Romans 2:14-15) and common

---

8. McGrath, *Bridge Building,* p. 49.

experience and is at the core of John Calvin's epistemology; especially as it is developed in *The Institutes of the Christian Religion*.

As McGrath states, '*The Institutes* is thus like a pair of spectacles through which Scripture may be properly read'[9] so to read Calvin is, as it were, to glean from the Bible. Calvin is painstaking in laying out his arguments in a clear and systematic way, building chapter upon chapter, exhaustively citing Scripture, until he has presented an argument that is virtually unassailable. Consequently, in Reformed circles, his writings are second only to the Bible itself as a reliable source for the investigation of sound theological principles.

Among those principles, we find the *sensus divinitatis*, itself positioned as a foundational element of Calvin's entire epistemological system.

> Our wisdom in so far as it ought to be deemed true and solid wisdom, consists almost entirely of two parts: the knowledge of God and of ourselves . . . But though the knowledge of God and the knowledge of ourselves are bound by a mutual tie, due arrangement requires that we treat of the former in the first place, and then descend to the latter (*Inst* 1.1.1).

But how, one may ask, is that possible for non-believers; for people outside of the covenantal community of faith who have no access to divine revelation? Calvin appears to anticipate such a question and explains right from the outset that consideration of the divine is, to a certain degree, possible for all human beings, by virtue of the fact that all human beings already possess within themselves an innate (if incomplete) knowledge of God. He states:

> That there exists in the human mind, and indeed by natural instinct, some sense of the Deity, we hold to be beyond dispute, since God himself, to prevent any man from pretending ignorance, has endued all men some idea of his Godhead . . . there has never been, from the very first, any quarter of the globe, any city, any household even without religion, this amounts to a tacit

9. McGrath, *Bridge Building*, p. 34.

confession, that a sense of Deity is inscribed on every heart (*Inst* 1.1.1).

This, Calvin claims, is an 'indisputable' fact which he bases on Romans 1:19 (where the Apostle Paul states that knowledge of God is 'evident' even to the unrighteous) and his observation of human beings as universal subjects of worship. Upon making this claim, Calvin immediately uses it apologetically, stating that:

> It is most absurd, therefore, to maintain, as some do, that religion was devised by the cunning and craft of a few individuals, as a means of keeping the body of the people in due subjugation . . . they never could have succeeded in this . . . had the minds of men not been previously imbued with that uniform belief in God, from which, as from its seed, the religious propensity springs (*Inst* 1.3.2).

It is interesting to note how relevant today are Calvin's words. It would appear that even in his day, there were those who subscribed to the notion that religion was, as Karl Marx later claimed, the 'opiate' of the masses; yet their arguments were as vacuous then as they are now. Calvin rightly observes (as did Aristotle, Augustine, Anslem and Aquinas before him), that religion and the very concept of God would in fact be 'inconceivable' were they not rooted in an ontological reality. He goes on to state that:

> All men of sound judgment will therefore hold, that a sense of Deity is indelibly engraven on the human heart. And that this belief is naturally engendered in all, and thoroughly fixed as it were in our very bones, is strikingly attested by the contumacy of the wicked, who, though they struggle furiously, are unable to extricate themselves from the fear of God (*Inst* 1.3.3).

It is interesting to see how Calvin, points to the behavior of the 'wicked' as proof that a certain knowledge of God universally exists. Despite our depravity as fallen human beings and despite the futile attempts of non-believers to mute the ever-present voice of their creator, at some point, every human being must come face to face with the reality of God; whether as an intellectual exercise or when faced with hardship or the prospect of our own mortality, the fear of God will ultimately take hold. And the purpose of instilling this fear, is not punitive, but redemptive. As Calvin clearly proclaims:

> I now contend—viz. that a sense of Deity is naturally engraven on the human heart, in the fact, that the very reprobate are forced to acknowledge it. When at their ease, they can jest about God, and talk pertly, and loquaciously in disparagement of his power; but should despair from any cause, overtake them, it will stimulate them to seek him, and dictate ejaculatory prayers, proving that they were not entirely ignorant of God, but had perversely suppressed feelings which ought to have been earlier manifested (*Inst* 1.4.4).

By establishing the foundational principle of the *sensus divinitatis*, Calvin has established a basis upon which one may build an intellectual case for the existence of God generally (*apologia*); and revelation of the Christian God specifically (*kerygma*). And so it is from this point in the *Institutes* that Calvin begins his exposition of the teleological proofs of God, in a fashion reminiscent of both Christian thinkers (Augustine, Aquinas, etc.) and pre-Christian thinkers (Socrates, Plato, Aristotle, etc.), followed by his exposition of the God of Scripture. Calvin is happy to present the veracity of the Christian world-view in the great marketplace of ideas and has no problem whatsoever defending the truth claims of Christianity on the 'common ground' of intellectual inquiry and the *sensus divinitatis*. As he notes in the *Institutes*:

> To charge the intellect with perpetual blindness so as to have in it no intelligence of any description whatever, is repugnant not only to the Word of God, but to common experience. We see that there has been implanted in the human mind a certain desire of investigating truth, to which it never would aspire unless some relish for truth antecedently existed (*Inst* 2.2.12).

And so for Calvin, this potent combination of an innate desire for truth and the *sensus divinitatis* provides a meeting point, a 'point of contact' as it were, between believer and non-believer; or to answer Tertullian, between Athens and Jerusalem; the Academy and the Church.

This theological premise is of fundamental import and comfort to those who seek to engage in the practice of Christian apologetics today; especially those who operate in a postmodern setting; where the rules of engagement have changed dramatically in recent years and long-held assumptions about God and truth are themselves undermined on a regular basis. In some ways, one may ask the question: 'What has Jerusalem to do with Oxford; Plato; Derrida and Western Pop-culture in the 21st Century'?

In the West, for most of the last twenty-five hundred years or so, two essential beliefs have been generally assumed. One is the belief that truth exists and should be sought after; and the second is the belief that a source of truth (i.e. God) exists and can, to a certain extent, be known. These may no longer be assumed. In fact, both have been seriously undermined in recent years and their weakening has made everything from the study of theology to the practice of apologetics much more difficult.

Belief in a personal God (as found in the Judeo-Christian tradition) has been especially singled out for attack since the so-called Age of Enlightenment with its epistemological emphasis on reason and cognitive proof. The nineteenth century in particular, with the publication of Darwin's *Origin of Species* and the philosophical writings of such men as Ludwig Feuerbach, Karl Marx, Sigmund Freud, Friedrich Nietzsche and many others, propagated a general belief that science alone was sufficient to answer life's big questions and that belief in God was merely 'wishful thinking' (Freud) or the result of 'cognitive malfunction' (Marx).

Of course, while no one can doubt the genius of modern science, it has hardly produced the sociological utopia that many philosophers of science had once predicted. In fact, many of the dystopian horrors of the twentieth century, from Hitler's Germany to the gulags of Russia; the development of nuclear weapons to global warming may, in some ways, be attributed to an over re-liance on the unbridled promises of modern science. Modern science is a very good servant, but a very bad master and while some in the scientific community would no doubt argue that science was not to blame for such atrocities, human beings were to blame; their very objection belies their all-encompassing faith in science and their belief system crumbles under its own weight. In short, science and scientists require the existence of non-scientific disciplines such as philosophy and theology, if for no other reason than to instill the moral codes necessary to regulate the potentially negative effects of scientific discoveries.

That is of course, unless one chooses to invent a biomechanical device that would explain away (in purely scientific terms) the phenomenon of moral choice and even the existence of God (or at least the existence of God as a concept). Such was the intent of Richard Dawkins when he penned his seminal work, *The Selfish Gene* in 1976 and created the now infamous 'meme' as an explanation of how human beings transmit cultural information across generations; including moral codes and religious beliefs. The 'meme' as he calls it (which is a monosyllabic abbreviation of *mimeme*, from the Greek *mimeomai*—to imitate) is a 'unit of cultural transmission, or a unit of imitation'.[10]

It is difficult to know where to start in critiquing Dawkins' theory of memes. Were he not a serious scientist (zoologist) and scholar (Charles Simonyi Professor for the Public Understanding of Science at Oxford University) one would be tempted to dismiss his theory as nothing more than an anthropomorphic description of a non-biological phenomenon (a bit like Adam Smith famously describing the phenomenon of self-correcting markets as an 'invisible hand'). However, Dawkins is a serious scientist and scholar and despite the fact that many of his fellow scholars have, over the last thirty years, seriously criticized meme theory as both unscientific and improbable (some calling it 'pseudo-science'), he has gained a wide, popular following among the general population and university students in particular. In *The Selfish Gene*, Dawkins treats God somewhat dismissively and without the anger

10. Richard Dawkins, *The Selfish Gene* (Oxford: Oxford University Press, 2006), p. 192.

and vitriol that would mark his later works, especially, *The Blind Watchmaker* and most recently, *The God Delusion*. In his earlier work he states the following:

> Consider the idea of God. We do not know how it arose in the meme pool. Probably it originated many times by independent 'mutation'. In any case, it is very old indeed ... The survival value of the god meme in the meme pool results from its great psychological appeal.[11]

This is a far cry from his later writings. As McGrath notes, by the time he publishes *The God Delusion* his position has hardened:

> God is a delusion—a 'psychotic delinquent' invented by mad, deluded people. That's the take-home message of 'the God Delusion'. Although Dawkins does not offer a rigorous definition of a 'delusion', he clearly means a belief that is not grounded in evidence—or, worse, that flies in the face of evidence. Faith is 'blind trust, in the absence of evidence, even in the teeth of evidence'. It is a 'process of non-thinking'. It is 'evil precisely because it requires no justification, and brooks no argument.[12]

One may ask why Dawkins has evolved into an 'atheist fundamentalist' or 'anti-theist' and why his writing has taken on such a militant tone. Perhaps he has been back-footed by the fact that his ideas have lost their luster in academic (if not popular) circles? Perhaps he finds it disconcerting to find eminent scientists from across various disciplines challenging not only his conclusions, but also the basic assumptions upon which he has formulated his thesis? Even world-renowned scientists are beginning to admit publicly that despite the genius of the scientific method, the physical sciences are limited in what they can and cannot explain. In many ways, the notion of the idea of God being a mental virus that has infected people represents a kind of 'contra-*sensus divinitatis*'; and so the debunking of Dawkins is important to the work of Christian apologists ministering to Generation Y. However, an even greater

11. Dawkins, *The Selfish Gene*, p. 192.

12 McGrath, Alister. *The Dawkins Delusion?* (London: SPCK, 2007), p. 1.

challenge to contemporary Christian apologists than Dawkins or anyone else arguing from a modernist perspective is the phenomenon of postmodern epistemology itself.

Space does not permit any more than a cursory definition of postmodernism, but McGrath defines it simply as an epistemological system with 'a pre-commitment to relativism or pluralism in relation to questions of truth'.[13]

On the one hand, a predisposition toward relativism and pluralism present a serious challenge to anyone presenting truth claims such as those offered by Christian apologists. How can we speak of truth to an audience predisposed to the notion that objective truth does not exist (or is at least unknowable)? McGrath suggests that:

> If the word 'truth' continues to cause intractable problems, an alternative approach may be tried. Instead of asking whether Christianity is *true*, the postmodernist might be asked whether it can be regarded as *credible*.[14]

Acknowledging that this is hardly a 'high road' approach, he laments:

> . . . sadly, the intellectual shallowness of much postmodernism perhaps obliges the apologist to stoop low in order to respond (to postmodernist objections).[15]

On the other hand, as Bridger rightly observes:

> From a postmodernist perspective, Dawkins and the other modernists have lost the very basis of their convictions . . . 'The self-confident days of rationalism have gone, to be replaced by deep *skepticism* about the claims of science to have unlocked the secrets of the cosmos or to have discovered reality in all its fullness . . . the cultural movement known as postmodernism has raised far more

---

13. McGrath, *Bridge Building*, p. 223.
14. McGrath, *Bridge Building*, p. 229.
15. McGrath, *Bridge Building*, p. 229.

radically skeptical questions about science than religious protagonists could ever have hoped to get away with.[16]

Ironically then, postmodernism may actually make it easier for Christian apologists to counter the arrogant claims of the scientific community (including the claims of Dawkins) to possess the only viable means of determining what is reasonable and what is true.

And so it would seem then, that armed with the conviction that all human beings do indeed possess a *sensus divinitatis* the contemporary Christian apologist can confidently engage in theological and philosophical discourse in a postmodern setting. In doing so however, one would do well to remember the probable epistemic bias of one's audience, including the challenges of both entrenched anti-religious sentiment and postmodern relativism. In practical terms, one may wish to consider the following issues:

1. Where should apologetic discussions take place? Are they best done in a formal, lecture room setting, or in a more casual setting, such as a local pub or coffee house?

2. How should the discussions be conducted? Is a pedagogical model appropriate, or would a dialogical method be more effective?

3. What topics should be addressed? Should the apologist spend a lot of time arguing for the 'reasonableness' of Christianity, or would it be more effective to address such 'potential defeaters' as: biblical authority; higher criticism; the person of Jesus; the problem of evil, etc.?

4. At what point does one present the Gospel? Is it the place of the apologist to invite people to consider Jesus personally or is it the role of the apologist to refer individuals to the Church for that purpose?

5. What is the role of prayer in the apologetic process? Does one pray openly (i.e. publicly) for individuals to come to a saving

16. Francis Bridger, *Why Can't I have Faith: working out dis-belief in the postmodern World* (London: Triangle, 1998), p. 31.

faith in Jesus Christ, or does one pray privately for the Holy Spirit to take people's general (and inadequate) knowledge of God to the next level?

6. How does one measure success? Or does one leave the results to God and focus instead on one's own obedience to Jesus' command to 'make disciples'?

These are all interesting and legitimate questions for the apologist to consider, however, at the end of the day, it is important to remember that God is ultimately in control of the process, as indeed he is in control of all things. As Calvin rightly reminds us:

> The general office of faith is, to assent to the truth of God, whenever, whatever, and in what manner so ever he speaks; but its peculiar office is, to behold the will of God in Christ, his mercy, the promises of grace, for the full conviction of the Holy Spirit enlightens our minds and strengthens our hearts (*Inst Aph.* 3.45).

This is good and heartening advice from the great Reformer and may prove particularly useful to Christian apologists when confronted by one of the most difficult and pervasive arguments against the existence of God: the age-old 'problem of evil'.

6

Covenant Theology and the Problem of Evil

A deranged young man walks into a small political gathering in Arizona and opens fire killing six people including a nine-year-old girl. Why? Two planes fly into the World Trade Center towers in New York City killing three thousand people. Why? An entire nation embraces a political ideology that results in the systematic extermination of six million Jews. Why? The day after Christmas an earthquake in the Indian Ocean triggers a tsunami that kills two hundred and fifty thousand people. Why? These aren't idle or impertinent questions, they are genuine, heartfelt and confounding questions that strike at the very heart of what it means to be human. 'Why do bad things happen to good people?' Or as A.T. Bledsoe put it so long ago:

> How under the government of an infinitely perfect Being, evil could have proceeded from a creature of his own, has ever been regarded as the great difficulty pertaining to the intellectual system of the universe.[1]

1. A.T. Bledsoe, *Theodicy; or Vindication of the Divine Glory* (New York: Nelson and Phillips, 1853), p. 11.

How indeed? How can an omnipotent, omniscient and omni-benevolent God allow such seemingly random acts of violence and suffering to occur with such regularity and on such a grand scale? Perhaps there is no God? Or worse still, perhaps God is as Richard Dawkins describes the God of the Bible:

> . . . a petty, unjust, unforgiving control-freak; a vindictive, bloodthirsty ethnic cleanser; a misogynistic, homophobic, racist, infanticidal, genocidal, filicidal, pestilential, megalomaniacal, sadomasochistic, capriciously malevolent bully'?[2]

As Christians we must of course reject both of these conclusions, the former on the grounds that it is heresy, the latter blasphemy. However, we must be both willing and able to offer a theodicy that is not only reasonable and useful for apologetic purposes, but one that is biblically sound and useful in pastoral situations as well.

In order to demonstrate how one may address these arguments in the context of Christian apologetics, I will set out below the basic arguments associated with 'the problem of evil' following the structure put forth by Professor Bart Ehrman in his recent book entitled: *God's Problem: How the Bible Fails to Answer Our Most Important Question—Why We Suffer* (2008). The reason for constructing an argument based on Ehrman's work is three-fold. Firstly he is a serious biblical scholar and church historian and as such cannot be disregarded as unfamiliar with the critical texts and/or the evolution of theodicy as a concept. Secondly while no longer a believer he is not an obnoxious 'anti-theist' in the mold of Richard Dawkins and his work is highly regarded by many thinking people. Thirdly, he is a very popular writer, and is often cited by skeptics in the context of Christian apologetics. After having critiqued Ehrman's views I will propose a response to his objections, consistent with the theological principles of covenant theology and briefly consider its apologetic and pastoral implications.

---

2. Dawkins, *The Selfish Gene*, p. 31.

GOD'S PROBLEM

As suggested above, questions surrounding the existence of evil and human suffering are not a recent phenomenon, nor are their consideration tertiary to our experience as human beings. As French theologian Henri Blocher once noted: 'While it is evil that tortures human bodies, it is the problem of evil that torments the human mind.'[3]

This certainly seems to have been the case for Ehrman, who in the opening chapter of his book relates the fact that while he was once a devout evangelical Christian, it was his inability to reconcile the existence of evil with his belief in the loving, all-powerful God of Christianity that ultimately brought him to a loss of faith. As he simply posits the problem: 'God is all powerful. God is all loving. There is suffering. How can all three be true at once'?[4]

Ehrman openly admits, that before coming to the conclusion that his faith in God and the existence of evil were irreconcilable, he was already beginning to doubt Christianity, largely because his academic study of the Bible had caused him to question its veracity (a topic that will be explored further, below). Consideration of the problem of evil however was the last straw.

His journey into theodicy began when he was asked to teach a course entitled: *The Problem of Suffering in the Biblical Traditions* at Rutgers University. There he exposed his students to some of the most widely known philosophers of religion (ancient and modern) who have attempted to solve this conundrum. He exposed them to the questions purportedly posed by the Greek philosopher Epicurus, the musings of David Hume and Gottfried Leibniz (who coined the term 'theodicy'), the literature of Voltaire and the works of more recent writers such as Eli Wiesel and Harold Kushner.

As he considered the various theories put forward by these great thinkers and compared them to the various biblical

3. Henri Blocher, *Evil and the Cross* (Downers Grove: Intervarsity, 1990), p. 1.

4. Bart Ehrman, *God's Problem: How the Bible Fails to Answer Our Most Important Question—Why We Suffer* (New York: HarperCollins, 2008–Kindle Edition).

approaches, he became frustrated by an apparent lack of symmetry to the arguments. According to Ehrman: ' . . . this presents a problem . . . because if in the end the question is resolved by saying that the answer is a mystery, then it is no longer an answer'.[5]

And so, unwilling to accept mystery as a suitable explanation for the co-existence of evil and an omnipotent, omniscient and omni-benevolent God, Ehrman concludes that there is no answer to the question; and seeks to make his point by revealing what he believes to be the Bible's unsatisfactory and often contradictory approaches to the problem.

The Classic View

Ehrman begins his treatment of the question as many have before him, by considering the horror of the Nazi Holocaust. He calls it 'the most heinous crime in the known history of the human race' and while that may or may not be true it is certainly a poignant and familiar example of corporate evil on a monumental scale. In order to stress his point, he describes many of the atrocities in considerable detail, as though doing so will somehow increase the efficacy of his argument. It is unnecessary. His point is clear. The question however remains the same: how can God allow such pain and suffering to take place, especially against his 'chosen people', the Jews? One explanation that Ehrman offers is what he describes as the 'classic view' found in most of the Old Testament and some of the New Testament, and he states that view quite bluntly: ' . . . people suffer because God wants them to suffer. And why does God want them to suffer? Because they have disobeyed him and he is punishing them'.

In order to support his hypothesis, Ehrman gives a nearly exhaustive recount of the history of the Jewish people from Moses to the destruction of the Temple in 587 B.C. He cites various texts from the Pentateuch and quotes liberally from the writings of the

5. Ehrman, *God's Problem*.

prophets (with special emphasis on Amos and Hosea). His conclusion is simply this:

> And so, as we have seen, the classical view of suffering permeates much of the Bible. It is found in the prophets, the book of proverbs, the historical books of the Bible and parts of the New Testament. In most of the Hebrew Bible, the view is thought to apply in the present life, in the here and now. Those individuals, groups, or nations that obey God and do his will, thrive; those who do not suffer. They suffer because God is punishing them for their sins.[6]

The suggestion is, according to Ehrman, that if only the people of Israel had turned from their sins and their idolatry and gone back to God, they would have been restored as a great nation and been blessed instead of punished. It would seem to Ehrman however that either their thinking was wrong or God didn't keep his end of the bargain. According to Ehrman:

> Still, there are the unfortunate historical realities. These predictions of future success and happiness never did come to fulfillment. Many people in ancient Israel did return to God, did abandon their worship of idols, did strive to follow God's laws, did keep their part of the covenant. But suffering never ceased and the utopian kingdom never arrived.[7]

This reality, according to Ehrman led the people of God to seek an alternative explanation to the problem of evil and suffering. The explanation is that suffering isn't God's 'punishment' for sin; it is merely the 'consequence' of human sin.

The Consequences of Sin

In this section of the book, Ehrman cites numerous examples of people in the Bible suffering as a direct result of the sin of others;

6. Ehrman, *God's Problem*.
7. Ehrman, *God's Problem*.

from the fratricide of Cain to the social dangers of transgressing the Decalogue, to the persecution of the early church. In every instance, the emphasis is placed on the fact that people make choices and those choices often produce negative consequences. He rightly observes that this view is strikingly similar to the 'free will defense' of Leibniz and others, but rejects it on one basic premise—it does little if anything to address the suffering caused by natural disasters (or 'acts of God'). Therefore, he concludes, there must be another explanation and that explanation is one that can also be found throughout the Bible—the concept of 'redemptive suffering'.

Redemptive Suffering

According to Ehrman: 'The idea that God could make something good come out of something evil, that salvation could emerge from suffering, eventually took a turn in the thinking of some of the ancient writers; a turn toward the suggestion that salvation in fact required suffering. This turn had already been made by the time we reach Second Isaiah . . . Second Isaiah speaks of the "servant of the LORD" who suffers on behalf of the people, and whose suffering in fact brings about God's salvation.'

This is a critical step in what Ehrman suggests is an evolution in the thinking of biblical authors as it relates to the problem of evil, and it becomes fundamental to Paul's understanding of the efficacy of the cross. Ehrman even goes as far as saying:

> This idea is found throughout the Bible, from Jewish scripture to the New Testament, starting with Genesis and continuing on all the way through the writings of Paul and the Gospels. In some ways it is the core message of the Bible: it is not simply despite suffering but precisely through suffering that God manifests his power of salvation . . .[8]

Ehrman goes on to claim that some aspects of this theory resonate with him and he shares a rather interesting chapter from

8. Ehrman, *God's Problem*.

his own life whereby his convalescence from a serious illness as a young man led him to a love of books (and ultimately his life's work—academic research). But in the end he rejects the concept of redemptive suffering because in his view, 'most suffering is not positive'. This then leads him to ask the question: 'does suffering make sense'? In his quest for a biblical answer he turns to two very different books—the books of Job and Ecclesiastes.

Job and Ecclesiastes

Ehrman's exegesis of Job is predicated on a two-author hypothesis. The theory being that the prose sections and the poetry section were written by two different people. This is not a unique hypothesis. However, what is unusual is Ehrman's conclusion that the two authors offer very different solutions to the problem of evil. Instead of viewing the narrative as a presentation of differing views of the problem as presented by Job, his friends and Elihu, that is ultimately answered sublimely by God himself, Ehrman insists that the two authors give distinctly different answers to the problem. The prose section, he contends presents the idea that suffering is a test of faith (a kind of variation on the redemptive theme), whereas the poetry section merely re-states the classic view outlined above. This does not sit well with Ehrman who states quite adamantly:

> As gratifying as the *Book of Job* has been to people over the ages, I have to say I find it supremely dissatisfying. If God tortures, maims, and murders people just to see how they will react—to see if they will not blame him, when he in fact is to blame—then this does not seem to me to be a God worthy of worship. Worthy of fear, yes; of praise, no.[9]

He then goes on to explore the book of *Ecclesiastes*; which I believe he totally misconstrues. However, the 'eat drink and be merry for tomorrow we die' element of *Ecclesiastes* thoroughly appeals to Ehrman and one is left wondering whether he is equally

9. Ehrman, *God's Problem*.

enamored with the nihilism of Friedrich Nietzsche. What appeals to him however, is not that the Judeo-Christian understanding of God can be reconciled with the existence of suffering; it's the suggestion that because Ecclesiastes doesn't put the blame for suffering on God, the best way to square the circle is to eliminate the existence of God altogether. From here Ehrman explores what he suggests is the final chapter in the 'evolution' of biblical thinking as it relates to the problem of evil and suffering: Judeo-Christian apocalypticism.

Judeo-Christian Apocalypticism

Ehrman's theory is based upon a simple hypothesis. Throughout the course of history, the God of the Bible has regularly intervened on behalf of Israel. This is done with the expressed intent of getting his people to turn away from their sin and idolatry, so that he can restore them to glory. However, when the people of Israel do eventually turn back toward God and the glory of Israel is not restored—in fact they face terrible persecution for their faithfulness—the religious leaders have a problem. They need to find another explanation for their predicament. The solution (according to Ehrman) is Judeo-Christian apocalypticism.

Fundamental to Ehrman's theory is a late writing of the *Book of Daniel*. Despite being set during the time of the Babylonian captivity, Ehrman (and many other biblical scholars) believe that the book was actually written at the time of the Maccabean Revolt some four hundred years later. According to proponents of this theory, during the Maccabean period, the traditional prophetic arguments about suffering being punitive simply didn't hold up. As he puts it:

> Here was a case of people suffering not because God was punishing them for breaking the Law but because God's enemies were opposing their keeping the Law. The old prophetic view seemed unable to accommodate the

circumstances. A new view developed, the one scholars today call apocalyptisicm.[10]

As Ehrman points out, the identifying features of apocalypticism are:

1. Dualism (i.e. it was the ancient Jewish apocalyptics who 'invented' the Devil).

2. Pessimism (i.e. it is beyond human capability to improve the lot of humanity).

3. Vindication (i.e. there will be a final judgment).

4. Imminence (i.e. 'the end is neigh').

From this thinking (according to Ehrman) the entire theological system of Judeo-Christian beliefs, as we understand them today, evolved. It gave us heaven and hell, life after death, Armageddon and most of all the incarnation and the cross. And Ehrman is not completely critical of it. He states:

> I find this very powerful and attractive. This is a view of the world that takes evil seriously . . . It is also a view designed to give hope to those experiencing suffering that otherwise seem too much to handle . . .[11]

Sadly, he doesn't find it to be *true*—especially the incarnation. He states quite clearly:

> The idea that God himself suffers is based on the theological view that Jesus was God . . . For me, it (the incarnation) is an interesting and important theological development, but not one that I find convincing.[12]

Instead, like the character of Ivan from Dostoevsky's *Brothers Karamozov*, he finds the whole enterprise of human suffering too overwhelming to be attributable to any concept of God that he

10. Ehrman, *God's Problem.*
11. Ehrman, *God's Problem.*
12. Ehrman, *God's Problem.*

would find appealing and so he sadly concludes that the dilemma is irresolvable.

While I respect Professor Ehrman's capabilities as a textual scholar, his arguments pertaining to the problem of evil put forth above are far from unassailable.

Ehrman's Problem—A Flawed Hermeneutic

Ehrman's difficulty as a theologian begins not with poor exegesis of biblical texts, but with a flawed hermeneutic. In short, Ehrman rejects the concept of a biblical meta-narrative. He states unequivocally that any attempt to read a modern message into a biblical text (especially prophesy) is 'egocentric'. In fact, he states categorically that: 'The prophets were not concerned about us; they were concerned about themselves and the people of God living in their own time'.

Referring specifically to the Book of Revelation, he states that: 'The Book of Revelation was not predicting what is going to happen in our own time. Its author was concerned with what was happening in his time'.

These are statements that not only betray Ehrman's flawed hermeneutic; it also illustrates his low view of scripture.

Ehrman's Problem—A Low View of Scripture

As Ehrman admits not only in this book, but also in *Misquoting Jesus*, a work specifically dealing with the nature of scripture:

> . . . my strong commitment to the Bible began to wane the more I studied it. I began to realize that rather than being an inerrant revelation from God, inspired in its very words . . . the Bible was a very human book with all the marks of coming from human hands: discrepancies, contradictions, errors, and different perspectives of different authors living at different times in different countries and writing for different reasons to different audiences with different needs. But the problems of the

Bible are not what led me to leave the faith. These problems simply showed me that my evangelical beliefs about the Bible could not hold up, in my opinion, to critical scrutiny.[13]

I find it quite remarkable that Ehrman doesn't appear to see the obvious flaw in his logic. He purports to be using the Bible as proof that the God of the Bible is inconsistent with the existence of evil and human suffering—yet he doesn't believe in the concept of revelation. If that is true, then the Bible cannot be relied upon to be an accurate representation of the Divine (even the divinity it purports to represent). He is therefore seeking to prove something about a subject (evil) and its relation to an object (God) whose information source is (in Ehrman's own opinion) unreliable. That is an epistemological as well as a theological problem for Ehrman.

Ehrman's Problem—An Aversion to Complexity

As alluded to earlier, Ehrman appears to prefer 'simple' solutions to complex problems. Who doesn't? Unfortunately, the so-called 'problem of evil' requires one to consider the mind of God and to contemplate questions that have baffled philosophers and theologians for centuries. Ehrman recognizes that there are modern theodicists, but he dismisses their work as:

> . . . precise, philosophically nuanced, deeply thoughtout, filled with esoteric terminology and finely reasoned explanations for why suffering does not preclude the existence of a divine being of power and love. Frankly to most of us these writings are not just obtuse, they are disconnected from real life.[14]

Coming from a scholar, I find such a sentiment to be nothing less than scandalous. It has taken humankind centuries to figure out that the world isn't flat, that cells divide, that matter consists

---

13. Ehrman, Bart. *Misquoting Jesus* (New York: HarperCollins, 2009—Kindle Edition).

14. Ehrman, *Misquoting Jesus.*

of molecules, that time isn't constant and that something called the Higgs-Boson Particle may actually exist. Surely the answers to these and countless other questions relating to the nature of our existence didn't come easily. The fact that the answer to a particular question may not be obvious; doesn't preclude the possibility of one eventually finding a suitable answer. Doing so however, may in fact entail the use of 'finely reasoned explanations'—at least one would hope so.

Ehrman's Problem—Flawed Christology and the Judgment of God

Ehrman clearly states above that he rejects the incarnation and this, in my view is at the root of his inability to see the uniqueness of the Christian faith as the only satisfactory answer to the so-called 'problem of evil'. In his chapter on Judeo-Christian apocalypticism he comes agonizingly close to realizing that in the cross one may see God not as the author of evil and suffering but as both a fellow sufferer and ultimate deliverer. Instead Ehrman suggests on several occasions that he finds the God of the Bible to be capricious at best and callous at worst. In this of course, he is not alone. As the late Pope John Paul II so rightly observed:

> The history of salvation is also the history of man's continual judgment of God. Not only of man's questions and doubts but of his actual judgment of God . . . But God, who besides being omnipotence is wisdom and love, desires to justify Himself to mankind. He is not the Absolute that remains outside of the world, indifferent to human suffering. He is Emmanuel, God-with-us . . . The scandal of the cross remains the key to interpretation of the great mystery of suffering which is so much a part of the history of mankind. Even contemporary critics of Christianity are in agreement on this point. Even they see that the crucified Christ is proof of God's solidarity with man in his suffering. God places himself on the side of man. He does so in a radical way. 'He emptied himself, / taking the form of a slave, / coming in human like-ness,

/ and found human in appearance, / he humbled himself, / became obedient to death, / even death on the cross' (Philippians 2:7-8). Everything is contained in this statement.[15]

Sadly, that is not how Bart Ehrman sees things.

Ehrman's Problem — No Room for a Federal System

Finally, there is no room in Ehrman's thinking for a federal system of atonement that would ultimately make sense of the current state of human affairs, the effects of evil and an ontological / eschatological resolution of the problem. That is because Ehrman rejects one of the most important elements of such a system—original sin. He states quite adamantly that:

> The first act of disobedience committed by human beings, of course, did not directly harm anyone else . . . The results of their disobedience were bad: they were driven from the garden (etc.) . . . But the results were punishment for their sin; the sin itself had no effect on anyone else.[16]

This position of course flies in the face of most Christian orthodoxy (although the Eastern Churches hold to a similar view), however, more importantly, it directly contradicts what the Bible teaches in Romans 5:12-21 and 1 Corinthians 15:22. This is tragic, as in my view there is no better way to reconcile the existence of evil and the existence of an omnipotent, omniscient and omnibenevolent God than the federal system commonly known as covenant theology.

15. John Paul II, *Crossing the Threshold of Hope* (New York: Alfred A. Knopf, 1994), p. 62.

16. Ehrman, *God's Problem.*

THE COVENANT PARADIGM—(SUZERAIN / VASSAL PROTECTION)

The *Dictionary of Scottish Church History and Theology* defines covenant theology as: 'the use of the covenant concept as an architectonic principle for the systematizing of Christian truth.' Professor Meredith Kline (whom I had the privilege of studying under) describes covenant theology as: 'biblical theology' and a 'meta-narrative' for the whole of scripture. Using ancient near-eastern suzerain / vassal treaties as a paradigm for God's relationship with his creation, proponents of covenant theology believe that it is possible not only to understand the nature of that relationship, but to understand as well, the meaning behind historic events—from creation to consummation.

I also believe that an understanding of covenant theology can provide a satisfactory framework for understanding the so-called 'problem of evil'. That is because the one universal principle common to all covenantal agreements is this: in exchange for fealty / obedience a suzerain promises to provide protection for a vassal. If one can understand the history of God's covenantal relationships with humankind, one can understand the pre-eminence of God's grace, even in the face of wide-scale human suffering.

In order to appreciate covenant theology, however, one must first understand the definition of a covenant. Kline calls a covenant 'a commitment with divine sanctioning'. More specifically however, Kline defines the divine covenants found in the Bible as 'divinely sanctioned administration(s) of God's kingdom'. According to the tenets of covenant theology, a covenant is any 'oath document' that includes a series of requisite 'blessing / curse' provisions. Divine covenants (as found in the Bible) however, are ones where God is both 'participant and enforcer' and whose efficacy is specific to God's sovereign purposes.

Generally speaking, there are three 'macro' covenantal formulas that cover the biblical meta-narrative. They are:

1. The covenant of redemption (*pactum salutis*), a pre-temporal, intra-Trinitarian covenant whereby God the Father accepts

in provectus, the sacrifice of the Son in fulfillment of the covenantal requirements of fallen humanity. It is a quintessentially pre-eminent act of redemptive grace.

2. The covenant of works (*foedus operum*), a temporal, pre-lapsarian, bi-lateral covenant between God and humankind, federally represented by the first human (Adam), whereby God promises the 'total protection' of humankind in exchange for fealty / obedience. The breaking of this covenant by Adam resulted in the fall of humankind (original sin) and the temporary withdrawal of God's umbrella of total protection.

3. The Covenant of grace (*foedus gratiae*), a series of temporal, post-lapsarian covenants between God and humankind, federally represented by individuals, families and nations. Under these covenants God temporarily provides humankind with 'partial protection'—until such time as the benefits of the aforementioned covenant of redemption are realized.

Under this construct of 'macro' covenants, there are many 'micro' covenants, such as: God's covenant with Adam after the fall; God's covenant with Noah; God's covenant with Abraham (and his descendants); God's covenant with Moses and the people of Israel (an act of grace but with a typology reminiscent of works—i.e. the Law), God's covenant with David, and of course the 'new covenant' in Jesus Christ—whereby the requirements of the covenant of redemption (with Christ as federal representative of humankind) are ultimately fulfilled and God's permanent umbrella of total protection is ultimately restored.

Covenant Theology as Biblical Hermeneutic

As mentioned above, one of Ehrman's biggest problems is his flawed hermeneutic. By denying the existence of a meta-narrative, Ehrman is unable to see the relationship between historical events, much less discern their significance in God's economy. Yet, the existence of a meta-narrative seems to me to be strikingly obvious.

From the opening chapters of Genesis, where God's creation is described as a series of suzerain / vassal relationships (i.e. days one through three establish the 'kingdoms' of: day/night, sea/sky and land; and days four through six establish their respective 'rulers': sun/moon, fish/birds and animals/man) to the Book of Revelation where God creates a 'new heaven and a new earth' and his kingdom is firmly and eternally established (Revelation 21)—the relationship between God and humankind is clearly that of suzerain and vassal(s) in covenant. The underlying ethic of that covenantal relationship is God's loving kindness and grace in the face of human rebellion.

Evil and the Covenant of Redemption

I cannot overstate the importance of the covenant of redemption in responding to the so-called 'problem of evil'. As Ehrman notes when he describes his loss of faith: 'I came to think that there is not a God who is actually involved with this world of pain and misery—if he is, why doesn't he do something about it'?

Unfortunately, this is not an uncommon lament. But of course, as the covenant of redemption establishes, God has *done* something about it. Before the foundations of the world were laid, God had already decided to respond to humankind's disobedience with grace (via the cross of Christ). As the Bible clearly states:

> You know that from your empty way of life inherited from your ancestors you were ransomed—not by perishable things like silver or gold, but by precious blood like that of an unblemished and spotless lamb, namely Christ. He was foreknown before the foundation of the world but was manifested in these last times for your sake (1 Peter 1:19-20).

This one passage alone reaffirms the reality of original sin (i.e. 'empty inheritance'), the need for redemption (i.e. 'ransom'), the paradigm of the temple system (i.e. 'spotless lamb'), the pretemporal nature of the Son (i.e. 'foreknown before the foundation of the world') and the efficacy of his sacrifice (i.e. 'manifested for your sake'). God had already decided to forgive humankind before the fall, however the fall and its affects are also fundamental to understanding the co-existence of evil and an omnipotent, omniscient and omni-benevolent God.

Evil and the Covenant of Works

One of the most remarkable things about Ehrman's exegesis of the Genesis account of the fall is his utter failure to acknowledge Adam and Eve's guilt or God's right to impose the ultimate sanction. Yet the Bible is explicitly clear about the wages of sin. Eve herself tells the serpent in the garden, that if they disobey God they 'will die' (Genesis 3:3) and Paul states clearly in the New Testament that 'the wages of sin is death' (Romans 6:23). But instead, Ehrman chooses to describe God's 'less than ultimate sanctions' as capricious, when in fact, it was perfectly within God's right (and in keeping with covenant principles) not only to impose the ultimate sanction on Adam and Eve, but to end the 'human experiment' altogether. However, God does not exercise his sovereign right to do so. Instead, he chooses to respond to Adam and Eve's disobedience with grace, love and patience—as he will continue to do throughout the biblical epoch.

Evil and the Covenant of Grace

As mentioned previously, the covenant of grace may be simply described as God deferring his sovereign right to sanction humankind *because* of its disobedience, in favor of forgiving humankind *in spite* of its disobedience. The overwhelming majority of the biblical narrative tells the story of a loving and gracious Father, constantly instructing, correcting, forgiving, and ultimately redeeming his wayward children. As mentioned above, God was under no compulsion (other than that which was self-imposed in the covenant of redemption) to pardon humankind after the fall, yet that is exactly what God chose to do.

An appreciation for the covenant of grace doesn't merely render Ehrman's treatment of the co-existence of evil and an omnipotent, omniscient and omni-benevolent God incorrect—it exposes it as perverse. Throughout his work, Ehrman betrays the fact that he is spoilt by grace. That is to say, he has benefited so much from God's grace that he confuses the remnant effects of humankind's folly, with evil intent on the part of God. He also seems to lack an appreciation for the fact that God exercised his grace without compromising his justice—by allowing the oblation for sin to be paid by himself in the person of Jesus Christ.

APOLOGETIC IMPLICATIONS–THE NATURE OF EVIL *(PRIVATIO BONI)*

Perhaps Ehrman's problem lies in his misunderstanding of the nature of evil itself? If so, he would not be the first person to do so. Evil, it would seem to Ehrman, comes from God. God is not only the agent of evil, he is the author of evil, and at times he appears gratuitous, either in his willful use of evil and suffering as tools in his arsenal of judgment, or in his callous refusal to intervene to stop its effects when the power to do so is within his purview. He is wrong.

As Reventlow and Hoffman note in their book entitled: *Problem of Evil and its Symbols in Jewish and Christian Tradition* (2004), there is a long-standing tradition within Christianity known as *privatio boni*; which is the belief (posited by Augustine and others) that evil is not the *opposite* of goodness—evil is the *absence* of goodness. While evil may be manifested in many ways, including the personification of evil commonly known as Satan, evil itself has no properties of its own and is not substantive. Evil is what is left when God is removed from the formula. Prior to the fall humankind was under the total protection of the Almighty and evil had no sway over it. Since the fall however, God's umbrella of protection is only partial and while God may choose to intervene in exceptional circumstances, he has promised that the current state of affairs is only temporary and that the day will come when: 'He will wipe every tear from their eyes. There will be no more death, or mourning or crying or pain, for the old order of things has passed away' (Revelation 21:4).

In the overall scheme of things, what more could Ehrman or anyone else for that matter, reasonably ask of God?

THE 'LOGIC' OF COVENANT THEOLOGY'S RESPONSE TO THE PROBLEM OF EVIL

Ehrman's motivation for writing his book is to present an argument against the existence of God—or at least the Judeo-Christian God. Without the benefit of covenant theology, one might conclude that his arguments are sound and that the existence of evil and suffering are incompatible with the existence of an omnipotent, omniscient and omni-benevolent God. However, I believe that the construct of covenant theology presents a perfectly logical paradigm for over-coming the so-called 'problem of evil'. The logic is as follows:

1. An omnipotent, omniscient and omni-benevolent being exists (called God).

2. God is the pre-existent source of all being and all that is 'of' God is good. All that is not of God is evil.

3. Human beings emanate from God and are subject to God's sovereignty.

4. Human beings have a duty of fealty and obedience to God as their source of being.

5. Fealty and obedience are administered by divine covenant.

6. Reward for fealty and obedience is total protection from the effects of evil and suffering.

7. The sanction for unfaithfulness or disobedience (covenant-breaking) is 'non-being'.

8. Human beings have broken covenant with God and are deserving of sanction.

9. God has graciously deferred sanction and only partially withdrawn protection.

10. Human beings continue to exist in a temporary state of partial protection and thereby experience the partial effects of evil and suffering.

11. God himself has provided an oblation for covenant breaking and promised a future and eternal state of total protection.

12. Therefore, the temporary existence of evil and suffering is not inconsistent with the existence of an omnipotent, omniscient and omni-benevolent God.

PASTORAL IMPLICATIONS

As Feinberg notes, when people are suffering many well-meaning Christians fail in their attempts to bring comfort:

> Invariably, people will try to say something they hope will help. Sometimes it does, but often it is extremely insensitive and only drives the sufferer further into despair . . . (such as): 'You know, if you were a Calvinist, you'd see that God is in control of all this, and then you could rest in Him'.[17]

This is not what I am suggesting! However, as Ehrman states in his consideration of Judeo-Christian apocalypticism (cited above), a theodicy that has pastoral value must 'take evil seriously'; and covenant theology does just that. It is also helpful to point out that:

• Not every evil that befalls us is our own fault (sometimes it is merely a result of our post-lapsarian existence).

17. J.S. Feinberg, *The Many Faces of Evil* (Grand Rapids: Zondervan, 1979), pp. 321-24.

- Sometimes (often, actually) God does exceptionally intervene to relieve suffering and those who seek relief are right in praying for it.

- Suffering can be redemptive.

- A loving and gracious God is ultimately in control.

- God, in the person of Jesus Christ stands in solidarity with us in our suffering.

- All suffering is only temporary.

- God has written the end of the story and in the end, good triumphs over evil.

I accept that the problem of evil is a serious theological consideration and don't profess to have 'solved it' above. However, if one views the Bible through the prism of covenant theology, it is possible to construct a logical and satisfactory explanation that is ontologically and eschatologically sound and useful in both apologetic and pastoral situations.

DEVELOPING APOLOGETIC SKILLS—CASE STUDY

As mentioned previously, the Oxford American Mission's weekly apologetics group was the brainchild of a graduate student, not the Chaplain. The suggestion was tabled because the young man felt as though he and his fellow Christian students were ill equipped to defend the Christian faith in casual settings. He was convinced that most Christian students are no longer trained in rhetoric and have trouble constructing lucid arguments according to generally accepted principles of logic ('first principles'). The idea was to form a group of students, tutors, pastors, etc. who would meet on a regular basis with the intention of honing their skills as apologists by challenging each other to defend the doctrines of Christianity against commonly held counter-arguments. While the discussions would be moderated by the Chaplain, the sessions would not be tutorials; they would be more dialogical than pedagogical, based on an iron sharpens iron approach.

And so the Oxford American Mission weekly apologetics group was formed with the expressed purpose of helping Christian students hone their rhetorical skills and become more confident apologists for the Christian faith.

The first set of discussions revolved around the basic principles of logic and helped students understand how to construct reasoned arguments, avoiding such pitfalls as circular reasoning, etc. The second set of discussions dealt with epistemology in general and the nature of religious truth claims in particular. Next the group examined the various arguments for and against the existence of God. Lastly, the discussions focused on specific areas of Christian doctrine, the nature of Christ, sin, redemption, salvation, etc. and whether or not those doctrines were indeed defensible and/or true.

The meetings took place every Thursday evening during term time and were held in the library of a nearby convent. The seating was soft and the chairs were arranged in a circular fashion and refreshments were served. All of this was done to make the setting as relaxed and informal as possible. The discussions usually began with a brief explanation of the topic being explored followed by general comments relating to the topic (i.e. why it is important, why it is under scrutiny, etc.). Then a 'Devil's Advocate' would start things in earnest by either assailing the basic premise as stated or by offering an opposing position. The students were then invited to defend the Christian position. The only rules were that the discussions must remain civil at all times and that arguments must be reasonably and logically constructed.

The apologetics group became very popular among a core group of students and was one of the regular activities most closely associated with the Oxford American Mission. It not only helped students become better apologists it provided a space for meaningful relationships to develop between the students, the Chaplain and each other.

It also led to a similar group being formed in cooperation with the Oxford University Secular Society. As described earlier, that group met on Saturday mornings and was called 'Breakfast with (insert the name of a theologian or philosopher)...'. Each academic year the writings of a Christian thinker were explored and the students (both Christians and non-Christians) would consider the merits of the works in question. In the first year of its existence, the group examined the works of Sorën Kierkegaard and it proved to be a very useful enterprise. So intrigued was the Chairman of the Secular Society that he requested the works of C.S. Lewis be examined the following year (this kind of activity is sometimes referred to as 'soft evangelism').

I believe that when properly constructed and presented, the truth claims of Christianity are compelling and are useful not only in defense of the Christian faith against its opponents, but as useful tools for evangelism as well.

APOLOGETICS AS PRE-EVANGELISM—CASE STUDY

'Pre-evangelism' may be defined as any activity designed to engage non-believers in dialogue with Christianity that is not in and of itself overtly evangelistic. The ministries of Francis Schaeffer, Ravi Zacharias and countless others would suggest that apologetics have a place in pre-evangelistic activities. In keeping with the tradition of apologetic, pre-evangelistic activities, the Oxford American Mission, the Graduate Christian Union and the Oxford Evangelical Pastorate have worked over the years on several pre-evangelistic events in Oxford, organized by a U.S. based organization called the Trinity Forum.

The Trinity Forum, founded by Christian author and social critic Os Guinness, is as its website states:

> ... a nonprofit organization that works to cultivate networks of leaders whose integrity and vision will renew culture and promote human freedom and flourishing. (They) provide access to a broad but focused body of classic and thoughtful writings designed to facilitate conversation and reflection around some of society's most intriguing questions and themes. This is accomplished

through unique programs and publications that offer
contexts for leaders to consider together the great ideas
that have shaped Western civilization and the faith that
has animated its highest achievements (Trinity Forum
2011).

The 'faith' referred to in the Trinity Forum preamble is of
course the Christian Faith and although the organization's aims
are not overtly evangelistic, it seeks to encourage future leaders to
consider the truth claims of Christianity and the contribution of
Christian thought leaders throughout the ages.

As the preamble to the OAM website states: 'every year
America sends over one-thousand of her "best and brightest"
students to study at Oxford University' (OAM 2011) and among
those are over one hundred Rhodes Scholars. Rhodes Scholars are
often 'thought leaders' in their fields who go on to positions of
great prominence and societal influence. However, they tend not
to be a particularly religious group and are not easily accessible to
ministries from outside the University. However, when a former
Rhodes Scholar, who was once a parishioner of mine, learned of
my plans to create the Oxford American Mission, he invited me
and other religious professionals to work with the Trinity Forum
to (as he put it), 'keep the rumor of God alive in Oxford'. I jumped
at the chance. Subsequently, we held several Trinity Forum events
in cooperation with the Rhodes community and I have to say they
were a highlight of the academic calendar.

The Trinity Forums held at Rhodes House often featured
high-profile public figures and speakers such as: Jonathan Ait-
ken, General Lord Dannet, Professor John Lennox, Os Guinness
himself and others, thereby guaranteeing high interest in the
events. The forums were a combination of keynote addresses and
breakout discussions based upon selected readings from the vast
array of Trinity Forum publications. The participants came from
a wide variety of faith traditions (or no faith tradition at all) and
vastly different cultures; and while the discourse was often intense
and even emotional, it was always thoughtful, courteous and at
times inspiring. After the main events (usually hosted during

Michaelmas Term) the chaplains of both the OAM and OEP were encouraged to host smaller, follow-up events in college (normally during Hilary Term) in the hope that relationships would continue to develop, mentoring would ensue, pastoral care, if needed would be offered and those who wished to explore Christianity further would have an opportunity to do so.

It's a model that worked well and one that I would encourage other people serving in secular environments to try. We held forums on topics as diverse as 'character in leadership', 'calling' and the 'problem of evil', and in every instance the moderators learned as much as the participants; but more importantly, personal relationships developed and the 'rumor of God' continued to grow.

APOLOGETICS AS EVANGELISM—CASE STUDY

While evangelism involves more than merely an intellectual exercise, I believe that a direct defense of Christianity in the marketplace of ideas can be a very effective tool in leading non-believers to positions of faith. In Oxford there are many organizations dedicated to this purpose, including the Zacharias Trust and the Oxford Centre for Christian Apologetics. In addition to the on-going work of those organizations, the Oxford American Mission, The Oxford Graduate Christian Union and the Oxford Evangelical Pastorate joined together every year to host a major University-wide event in cooperation with the Veritas Forum.

Unlike the Trinity Forum, the Veritas Forum is overtly evangelistic (and Evangelical). As their website clearly states:

> Veritas Forums are university events that engage students and faculty in discussions about life's hardest questions and the relevance of Jesus Christ to all of life. (They) seek to inspire the shapers of tomorrow's culture to connect their hardest questions with the person and story of Jesus Christ . . . (Their) forums address the difficult questions of life: What is freedom? What is forgiveness? Do our lives have meaning? Can reason and faith coexist? How can God allow suffering? Why should we care about

injustice? Why do religions seem to cause so much violence? How can we live a good life? Who is Jesus (Veritas 2011)?

The events hosted by OAM, OEP and GCU have been opportunities for leading Christian apologists to clearly and unabashedly state the truth claims of Christianity, whether in the form of an inter-faith round table discussion featuring such prominent figures as Professor Tariq Ramadan and Bishop Nazir Ali or in a head to head debate between the likes of Professor Robert Haldane and the late Christopher Hitchens.

While one cannot measure the success of such events, they have become part of the fabric of Christian apologetics in Oxford and as such are adding to the work of the Kingdom among graduate students. There are many such organizations and resources available to people seeking to reach Generation Y and I would highly recommend their use as tools for evangelism.

7

Mentoring Tomorrow's Leaders

For better or worse, it would seem as though churches and ministries today have a tendency to apply emerging business practices to their ministry programs in a naïve and often uncritical way. It is not uncommon to hear local consistories discuss the benefits of employing such innovations as targeted marketing; business process re-engineering; focus groups; and value-added services in an attempt to improve their church's 'effectiveness'. While I don't object to such tactics in principle, I do question whether they are as appropriate to the task of Christian ministry, as their proponents would sometimes suggest.

One such area of interest however, that has found its way from the Board Room to the Consistory Room and that I find very useful as a tool for ministry is mentoring. Mentoring is big business with corporations spending millions of dollars each year on programs designed to pass effective knowledge from one generation of management to the next. It has become a fundamental part of many companies' HR processes and is used in many non-business sectors as well, including the Church. The fact that a strategy works in the corporate world however does not automatically mean that it is suited to the Church; so in this chapter I will examine the phenomenon of mentoring ministry; explore how it may be defined;

how it may work in praxis; whether or not it is based upon sound biblical principles (and/or examples); and if found to be appropriate, how it might be applied in a postmodern setting.

DEFINING MENTORING MINISTRY

As Sunil Gupton (2006) rightly observes, mentoring is not a uniquely Christian activity. On the contrary, the term itself harkens back to Ancient Greece and Homer's *Iliad*, where a character by the name of Mentor acts as a kind of father figure to Telemachus, son of Odysseus, King of Ithaca. However, while one may cite countless examples from outside the Christian tradition, such as Socrates and Plato; Plato and Aristotle; Haydn and Beethoven; Freud and Jung; just to name a few, the biblical examples described below would suggest that there is indeed a place for mentoring ministry in the Church at large and as I have personally experienced, in ministering to Generation Y, especially.

John Mallison in his book entitled, *Mentoring to Develop Disciples and Leaders (1998)* defines Christian mentoring as 'a dynamic, intentional relationship of trust in which one person enables another to maximize the grace of God in their life and service'.[1] By 'dynamic', Mallison seems to suggest that mentoring relationships are by definition in a constant state of flux. They evolve over time as the individuals involved grow in relationship to each other and more importantly their relationships with God. They are intentional relationships in that they involve more than just serendipitous contact. Mentors actively seek out opportunities to positively affect the spiritual lives of less mature Christians, whether formally or informally. They are trust-based relationships, where the parties involved have the confidence to be vulnerable with each other and where there is an indissoluble assumption of confidentiality. They are relationships specifically designed to enable (i.e. equip, embolden, encourage) a person to maximize the grace of God not only in their own lives, but in turn, the lives of others (i.e. via a life

---

1. John Mallison, *Mentoring to Develop Disciples and Leaders* (Milton Keynes: Scripture Union, 1998).

of Christian service). It is a powerful and very challenging definition of mentoring ministry.

Horsfall (2008) cites some other simple, yet useful definitions as well. Rick Lewis, he notes defines Christian mentoring as 'promoting the work of God in the life of another'. Eugene Peterson (1999), using the term 'spiritual direction' synonymously with mentoring ministry, defines it as 'two people agree(ing) to give their full attention to what God is doing in one (or both) of their lives and seek(ing) to respond in faith'. Bruce Demarest (2003) refers to it as 'structured ministry in which a gifted and experienced Christian . . . helps another believer to grow in relationship and obedience to Christ'.

In these and countless other definitions certain principles appear to be absolute:

1. The person doing the mentoring must him/herself be a mature Christian. A certain degree of life experience and knowledge of the Faith are implied in the exercise.

2. The individuals involved must form a relational bond. This is not something to be done at arms-length. Mentors must be willing and able to engage others on a spiritually intimate level.

3. A conscious effort must be made to assist in the spiritual growth of one of the parties involved.

4. The relationship must God-centered.

5. The desired result should be a fruit-bearing Disciple of Jesus Christ.

MENTORING MINISTRY IN PRAXIS

Mallison, Horsfall, Guptan (2006), Kerry and Mayes (1995), Fenton (1998), and others, all approach the subject in a similar fashion. They each examine the personal attributes or qualities of a good mentor; the skills required to be effective in mentoring ministry and the various pastoral roles a mentor fulfills (as demonstrated in the lists below).

Personal Attributes:

- Mature Christian
- Knowledgeable
- Wise
- Experienced
- Credible
- Empathetic
- Compassionate / Loving
- Vulnerable
- Non-Judgmental Self-aware
- Modest
- Approachable
- Trustworthy
- Available
- Discreet

Required Skills:

- Communication
- Active Listening
- Focus
- Patience
- Able to Lead by Example
- Hospitality
- Able to Teach

- Criticize Constructively

- Foster Accountability

- Counseling

- Ability to Forgive Others

- Ability to Inspire Others

- Ability to Empower Others

Pastoral Roles:

- Pastor / Elder

- Preacher / Teacher

- Advocate

- Advisor

- Counselor

- Disciplinarian

- Confessor

- Pardoner

- Parent-figure

In the following section, I will explore some of the more salient features of these attributes in more detail.

Personal Attributes

As the Apostle Paul notes, a church leader should 'not be a recent convert' (1 Timothy 3:6), but instead (as stated earlier), a Christian mentor must him/herself be a 'mature Christian'. That is to say, they must themselves have experienced many of the same feelings and emotions, doubts and fears that less mature Christians experience early on in their journey of faith. A good mentor however, will have come through many of the trials that new believers experience with a stronger faith in the Lord than when they first gave their lives to Christ.

A good Christian mentor will be knowledgeable on several levels. First, they will know the Bible and the primary doctrines of the Faith. While mentors need not be biblical or theological scholars, they should know the Word of God sufficiently to demonstrate its efficacy as the believer's only standard of faith and practice. Likewise, mentors should be fluent enough in the fundamental doctrines of the Christian Faith to give guidance and assurance to new believers when they ask the challenging questions that will inevitably arise in the course of one's mentoring relationship. That is not to say that Christian mentors should have pat answers to all of life's difficult questions. On the contrary, one of the fundamental benefits of mentoring ministry is the development of a new generation of Christians with the tools and direction necessary to work things out for themselves. However, when it comes to confessional issues about the nature of God, sin, redemption and the like, mentors should be able to explain those doctrines in a clear, succinct and convincing manner. Mentors should also be knowledgeable about a mentoree's personal situation; their current circumstances; their upbringing; their profession and/or other fields of interest. Nothing builds empathy better than conveying a genuine interest in another person's life and circumstances.

Mentors however must be more than merely knowledgeable; they must also be wise. In an age of information overload, and postmodern epistemology, it would appear that wisdom has lost its cache. However, to a believer, wisdom is far more important and desirable than the world would have one believe. As the Book of Proverbs self-declares, they are:

> . . . for attaining wisdom and discipline; for understanding words of insight; for acquiring a disciplined and prudent life, doing what is right and just and fair; for giving prudence to the simple, knowledge and discretion to the young—let the wise listen and add to their learning, and let the discerning get guidance—for understanding proverbs and parables, the sayings and riddles of the

wise. The fear of the Lord is the beginning of knowledge,
but fools despise wisdom and discipline (Proverbs 1:2-7).

Such is the very aim of mentoring ministry and so mentors must themselves be wise. Mentors must also be people of experience, credible people for whom others will have respect and admiration. It makes no sense for a person to try mentoring someone else if they themselves have not experienced any of the things a mentoree is experiencing. That would be like someone who has never played golf trying to teach someone else how to play the game. They may enjoy the occasional trip to the driving range, but the outcome would be quite unsatisfactory.

Mentors should also be compassionate for that is a quality that most closely resembles the nature of Jesus Christ himself. To be compassionate, one must truly and genuinely care about the wellbeing of others.

Mentorees must never been seen as projects but as people with feelings and needs; hopes and desires; as real and as important as the mentor's. Throughout the Scriptures we see example upon example of Jesus performing acts of healing and other acts of mercy and kindness because he felt compassion for the people, such as the feeding of the four thousand (Matthew 15:32); giving sight to the blind (Matthew 20:34) and healing a leper (Mark 1:41).

A good Christian mentor should never be clinical about their relationship with a mentoree. They should be both willing and able to 'laugh with those who laugh and weep with those who weep'. In order to do this effectively however, mentors must be willing to be vulnerable themselves. Mentorees identify more closely with mentors who are real than with those who pretend to be invulnerable. The image of the 'wounded healer' is a powerful one, especially when applied to the Christ-paradigm that all good Christian mentors should seek to emulate.

Christian mentors must also be non-judgmental in their dealings with mentorees. That is not to say that mentors should not or must not provide moral instruction or even the occasional rebuke. They should and must do so if required. However, such instruction and/or rebuke must always be done for remedial and never putative purposes. It is the role of the mentor to correct a mentoree from time to time, but never to condemn.

Christian mentors should also be self-aware in that they should have a realistic understanding of their own talents and abilities as well as their own failings and shortcomings. This will inevitably lead to a healthy sense of humility on the mentor's part, which in turn is a useful weapon against excessive pedagogy.

Additionally, good Christian mentors must be approachable; trust-worthy; available and discreet. They must be approachable in the sense that they must not convey a position of such high rank and stature that potential mentorees will be too intimidated to establish a meaningful relationship with them. They must be trust-worthy because mentorees take considerable risks in exposing themselves to the scrutiny, nurture, and potential discipline of mentors and of course, confidentiality is fundamental to effective mentoring ministry.

Mentors must be available and willing to invest the time necessary to impact another person's life for their benefit and the benefit of God's kingdom. Lastly, mentors should be discreet in their dealings with mentorees. It need not be public knowledge that a particular person has been taken under the care of a particular mentor, unless that public knowledge was to serve some useful purpose to the mentoree. Relationships and associations when taken out of context can often be confusing to the casual observer affecting reputations in a negative manner. While secrecy is neither required nor desired, discretion should normally be the order of the day.

Required Skills

In order to be an effective mentor, one needs to possess certain skills essential to the undertaking, with communication skills being paramount among them. Much of the published research suggests that those mentors who communicate clearly with their mentorees are not only more successful in the end, they (and their mentorees) are happier during the process. Being able to clearly express how one feels, what one is thinking, what is expected of the other person are all critical elements of good mentoring. Also important is what Horsfall describes as 'active listening'. Active listening, he states is:

> . . .(the) ability to truly 'hear' what another person is saying (or sometimes not saying). . . and not merely 'waiting for our turn to speak'. In order to be a good 'active listener', one must 'focus consciously' on what the other person is saying . . . to shut out (one's) own thoughts . . . not to interrupt . . . (and) be comfortable with . . . silence.[2]

A good sign that a mentor isn't truly listening to their mentoree is a lack of questioning on the mentor's part. Good listening will almost always involve questions of clarification (in order to ensure that one has heard and understands correctly what the other person is saying) as well as open-ended, probing questions (designed to encourage deeper reflection on the mentoree's part and/or to challenge a mentoree's assumptions, opinions, etc.).

Next, a Christian mentor must be able to focus on the needs of their mentoree and not give short shrift to their time together. Lack of focus is not uncommon in superior / subordinate relationships, however it is a genuine sign of disrespect and mentorees will resent such treatment if it becomes evident. If a mentor does not have the time or the inclination to give their full attention to a mentoree then they should probably not be engaged in mentoring at all. Mentorees will remember how they were treated, long after they have forgotten much of what a mentor may have said. At the end of the day, the quality of the relationship is as important as the information imparted.

Of course, the other side of the coin to focus is patience. It is not easy being a mentor, of any kind and Christian mentoring is no different. One of the most difficult aspects of mentoring is having the patience to deal with the elementary nature of mentorees' questions, attitudes, behavior, mistakes or even their seeming

---

2. Tony Horsfall, *Mentoring for Spiritual Growth* (Abingdon: Bible Reading Fellowship, 2008).

inability to comprehend / work-through what may have become second nature to the mentor.

We sometimes forget however that we too were learners once and we tested the patience of the mentors in our own lives. An excellent example of the kind of patience required in mentoring ministry is the example of Jesus himself when dealing with the Disciples (especially it would seem, Peter). On countless occasions in the Gospels we see Jesus having to explain things in a detailed (almost elementary) way; and often having to repeat himself or having to reinforce one particular point or another. Never losing patience however, he continued throughout his earthly ministry (even after his resurrection) to reinforce his points in order to ensure the Disciples ultimately 'got it'. One such example is his admonition to Peter at the end of the Gospel of John:

> When they had finished eating, Jesus said to Simon Peter, 'Simon son of John, do you truly love me more than these?' 'Yes, Lord,' he said, 'you know that I love you.' Jesus said, 'Feed my lambs.' Again Jesus said, 'Simon son of John, do you truly love me?' He answered, 'Yes, Lord, you know that I love you.' Jesus said, 'Take care of my sheep.' The third time he said to him, 'Simon son of John, do you love me?' Peter was hurt because Jesus asked him the third time, 'Do you love me?' He said, 'Lord, you know all things; you know that I love you.' Jesus said, 'Feed my sheep' (John 21:15-17).

Jesus of course knew Peter well and knew of his propensity to forget or even ignore his teaching. On this occasion however, the stakes were too high and so Jesus patiently reinforced his message so that Peter would not forget his words after he was gone. Peter was quite a slow learner, but thanks to the patience (and other qualities) of his mentor, once he got it, he helped to bring redemption to the world.

Words however are simply not enough; in order to be an effective mentor one must be able to lead by example as well. This may in fact, be the one aspect of mentoring ministry that most clearly separates it from other forms of teaching. Mentors are by definition walking the walk, not merely talking the talk. They demonstrate in their own lives (their personal devotion, Bible reading, prayer life, comport, reputation, etc.) a biblical model of Christian discipleship. They are imitators of Christ who by their own example become models of Christian living. This principle was firmly established by the Apostle Paul in his instructions to his protégé Titus on the importance of picking people of high moral character and reputation for positions of leadership in the Church. Paul states quite clearly:

> An elder must be blameless, the husband of but one wife, a man whose children believe and are not open to the charge of being wild and disobedient. Since an overseer is entrusted with God's work, he must be blameless—not overbearing, not quick-tempered, not given to drunkenness, not violent, not pursuing dishonest gain. Rather he must be hospitable, one who loves what is good, who is self-controlled, upright, holy and disciplined. He must hold firmly to the trustworthy message as it has been taught, so that he can encourage others by sound doctrine and refute those who oppose it (Titus 1:6-9).

Nearly the entire passage deals not so much with what an elder knows (although that is addressed toward the end of the passage), but with how an elder conducts one's self. Leading by example is fundamental to all leadership positions in the Church and that would include those engaged in mentoring ministry.

Next (and also mentioned in the above referenced verse) is the importance of hospitality in mentoring ministry. In order to establish a relationship that is more than clinical and more than casual, a mentor must take the time to truly get to know a mentoree and vice versa. When practical, this happens best inside a mentor's home.

Here, a mentoree can get a genuine look inside a mentor's life. One's home says a great deal about a person (what things they value, how they express themselves, what books they read, how ordered their lives are, etc.) and opening up such a private place to a mentoree says something about their importance to the mentor as a person. Mentors need to be more than just friends, but friendship is a part of what it means to be a mentor and hospitality is an expression of genuine friendship. In fact, the Apostle Paul clearly implores the Church in Rome that they are to 'practice hospitality' (Romans 12:13) as did the Apostles Peter (1 Peter 4:9) and John (3 John 1:8).

Mentors must also be able to teach and to constructively criticize their mentorees, not to embarrass them or to demonstrate their own superior knowledge, but in order to help them grow in their Christian life. The source of a Christian mentor's knowledge of course, must be the Scriptures themselves, which are as Paul says, 'God-breathed and . . . useful for teaching, rebuking, correcting and training in righteousness, so that the man of God may be thoroughly equipped for every good work' (2 Timothy 3:16-17). Using the word of God as a tool in this way, enables a mentor to foster accountability on the part of a mentoree and hold them to a godly (biblically-based) standard of conduct.

A good mentor will also be a good counselor; not merely in the nouthetic sense as described in a previous chapter, but in both an empathetic and a cognitive way; helping mentorees to work-through their personal issues.

Lastly, effective Christian mentors must be able to forgive, inspire, and empower mentorees, releasing them to become the best disciples they can become. Jesus himself demonstrated these skills and employed them to great effect. One need only consider the story of the woman caught in the act of adultery' (John 8:1-11) to appreciate the power of forgiveness, inspiration and empowerment or his dealings with the woman at the well (John 4:1-42). In both cases Jesus shows exceptional grace toward the women, freeing them from their guilt, inspiring them to lead new lives and then sending them on their way to do just that. In many ways this is exactly what good discipleship is all about.

Pastoral Roles

In my humble opinion however, (and this is an opinion supported by the work of Greenslade(1967); Demarest(2003); and

Horsfall(2008), the first and most important role of a Christian Mentor is that of pastor (with a small 'p'). While a mentor has a role distinct from that of an ordained church leader (Pastor with a capital 'P'), he or she still needs to possess good shepherding skills, such as those outlined by Greenslade (1967). He or she must be willing and able to guide their mentoree(s) along a path of holiness in a pagan society; to nurture their mentoree(s) in preparation for a life lived according to God's values as opposed to the world's values.

Similarly, a good Christian mentor should as Thomas Oden (1982) suggests, be involved in the 'cure of souls' and the care of those in physical, mental, emotional, and spiritual need. He or she should be an elder in the generic sense (as opposed to the ecclesial sense) and bring his or her life experience to bear in a positive, instructive, and affirming way.

Mentors are teacher / preachers, even if that teaching / preaching is taking place, not from a pulpit, but in small intimate settings, not weekly but whenever and wherever opportunities present themselves. So too, Christian mentors are advocates, advisors, and counselors, offering guidance in areas effecting every aspect of a mentoree's Christian life; and when and where appropriate, even going to bat for the mentoree when they need a little extra help and can't quite succeed otherwise. Jesus tells us that we all must 'carry our crosses and follow him' (Luke 14:27 para.), but every now and then we need help carrying our crosses, as Jesus himself required on the road to Calvary (Matthew 27:32).

As suggested above however, the mentor must also (at times) be a disciplinarian, a confessor and a pardoner. These sacerdotal roles are extremely important because Christian mentors are fulfilling a kind of parent-figure role; acting as God's own surrogates in the nurture and development of new believers. When they rebuke, when they correct and when they pardon (whether privately or in some cases as part of a judicial process) they do so not by their own authority but on behalf of God and the Church.

MENTORING MINISTRY IN THE BIBLE

While mentoring ministry *per se* is not specifically described as such in the Bible, it would appear that ministry of this type is attested to in many relationships throughout the Scriptures. One such relationship is that of Jethro and Moses.

Jethro was not only Moses' father-in-law; he was also a priest of Midian (Exodus 3:1) and a man of considerable wealth and power. In his relationship with Moses he demonstrated many of the aforementioned personal attributes and skills associated with mentoring ministry. He was hospitable, he was patient, he was wise and he was willing to give counsel to Moses at a time when Moses needed that counsel. One need only look at the events described in Exodus Ch. 18 to see what a good mentor Jethro was to Moses.

First, after hearing of the great deeds that God had done for the people of God in their escape from Egypt, Jethro immediately ensured that the focus remained on God by offering a sacrifice and inviting the key leaders of the community to participate in the event. As alluded to earlier, keeping things God-centered is fundamental to good mentoring.

Afterwards, Jethro observed Moses as he dealt with the people as their chief administrator. Jethro saw that sitting all day in the judgment of petty disputes was not the best use of Moses' time and talents nor was it good for his health and so he advised him (wisely so) to do several important things:

1. He encouraged him to accept his rightful place as a priest, a representative of the people before God.

2. Then he empowered him to teach the people God's commands and to implore them to obey the Lord and do what was right in his sight.

3. Lastly, he instructed him to appoint subordinate administrators to decide the lesser matters themselves, thereby freeing Moses to concentrate on more important duties.

After hearing the advice of his father-in-law, Moses had a choice; he could have either accepted the counsel of the older, wiser, and more experienced man, or he could have ignored the advice and gone his own way. He wisely chose the former, thereby freeing himself to seek God in the deserts of Sinai. Afterwards, Jethro returned to his home and we never hear of him again, however his role as Moses' mentor was finished. Soon it would be Moses' turn to mentor Aaron.

Simply put, Aaron was Moses' protégé from the beginning. He was with Moses throughout the major events described in the Book of Exodus from their calling by God to confront Pharaoh (Exodus 4:27); to the confrontations themselves (Exodus Chs. 5-11); to the first Passover (Exodus 12:21-28); to the crossing of the Red Sea (Exodus 14:1-31) to the receiving of the Law (Exodus 19:24); to the sealing of the Covenant (Exodus 24:1- 11) Aaron was there. He and his progeny were singled out by God to serve as priests (Exodus 28:1-14) and he was personally consecrated by Moses as a priest according to the instructions that God had given to Moses (Exodus 29:1-37 / Leviticus 8:1-36).

In all of these situations we see the same pattern; God speaks to Moses directly and Moses then passes on the Word of God directly to his mentoree, Aaron. However, things did not always go smoothly. In one instance in particular, when Aaron was left in charge of the people as Moses' surrogate, Aaron failed in his duties as a leader with catastrophic consequences. Exodus Ch. 32 tells the story of Aaron allowing himself to be bullied by the people and instead of standing firm against them (as leaders are sometimes called to do) he indulged their disobedience and allowed them to make a golden idol (calf) which they worshipped as a God. When Moses first learned of their transgression he immediately appealed to God for mercy on their behalf (Exodus 32: 11-14), as a good mentor often will. However, when he witnessed their sin with his own eyes, he became furious (even smashing to pieces the tablets of the Law) and disciplined them in the most severe fashion - not to merely punish them, but to restore them; eventually asking again that God show mercy upon them (Exodus 32:19-32). Afterwards the people are expelled from Sinai and Moses takes control of the community again; but in time Aaron and the priests were restored and Moses himself re-consecrated Aaron and his sons to their priestly office (Exodus 40: 12-16).

In all of these events we see Moses acting as mentor and Aaron as mentoree. We can witness the closeness of their relationship; the admiration and affection they have for each other; the wisdom that is shared; the assistance that is given; the empowerment that is executed; the rebuke and painful correction that is necessary in order for restoration to take place and for Aaron to ultimately take his place of authority in the community. But mostly, we see the God-centered nature of their entire relationship. This pattern will continue throughout the Scriptures as we see example upon example of mentors nurturing, preparing, and grooming others for a life of service to the Lord.

Some other notable examples include: Moses and Joshua (Exodus) Deborah and Barak (Judges) Naomi and Ruth (Ruth) Eli and Samuel (1 Samuel) Samuel and David (1 Samuel) Elijah and Elisha (1 & 2 Kings) Jesus and His Disciples—Especially Peter, James and John (Gospels) Paul and Timothy and Titus (Acts / Epistles), just to name a few. In fact, it is difficult to read the Bible and not conclude that mentoring ministry is a biblically based enterprise.

MENTORING MINISTRY TO GENERATION Y

Working in any chaplaincy situation has its unique challenges. When one is a chaplain they are a representative or more accurately an ambassador of the Church in a secular environment. When working as a chaplain in a university (such as Oxford University) where postmodern thinking and anti-theism are widespread however, one is not merely operating in a secular (i.e. neutral) environment, but (at times) in an openly hostile environment. There was a time when chaplains could simply post the dates and times of Bible studies or worship services and reasonably expect students to come in considerable numbers. That is simply no longer the case. Now one needs to seek other ways in which to influence students and hopefully instill in them knowledge of, and an appreciation for, God's Word. Mentoring ministry is one such method that may be usefully employed, especially when working with more mature students.

In my own experience as someone new to the University, I had to establish my credentials as a potential mentor. This was accomplished on three levels, first in my capacity as an ordained minister, then as an academic and lastly as an experienced international business executive. The latter had to do with the fact that I had spent over 25 years working in corporate settings and held senior positions with large companies and run large, complex organizations. Before arriving in Oxford I assumed that experience would be the least interesting to students. I was wrong. In fact, as both clergy and academics are in ample supply, it was my business experience that students found most useful. Many of them had little exposure to people in the business world and they enjoyed picking the brain of someone who had sat in the corner office. In fact, my rather unusual combination of experiences has proven to be of interest to a broad cross-section of post-graduate students and has resulted in my being able mentor to several of them.

MENTORING MINISTRY—A TRUE STORY

In many ways Josh was a 'typical' Oxford post-grad. He had come from a privileged background and attended a well-known boarding school. He did his undergraduate degree at Harvard, followed by a Masters degree in physics at Cambridge. When I met him he was doing a DPhil in Chemistry. As with most post-graduate students he had a tough workload that included as many hours in the lab as in the library (not to mention responsibilities as a newly married husband). He also came from a family where the expectation of success was palpable. It was a very difficult and stressful time and his young family was feeling the strain. During the first year of his degree his marriage fell apart and his wife left him, returning to the United States. He was devastated and while he had a small circle of friends he had no real church life per se and he needed a Christian mentor. My first contact with Josh (as with most of the students

I've worked with in Oxford) was made at a weekly GCU event; but soon after, he asked whether we could meet one on one, in order to help him work through his many complex issues.

In the beginning of our relationship, my role with Josh was more pastoral than anything else as I tried to help him take personal responsibility for his own part in the failure of his marriage. Work, I warned him, (whether in business, the academy or any other field) can be a very jealous mistress and if well-intentioned people such as he are not careful, they can find themselves being unfaithful to their spouses—emotionally, if not physically. The result of this unfaithfulness can be the destruction of a young marriage and Josh needed to understand the difference between having a healthy desire to succeed and an all-encompassing lust for success. In addition to helping him work through these issues from a pastoral perspective however, I was also able to share with him experiences from my own life in the corporate world where I have seen countless executives sacrifice everything from their families to their own physical and mental health on the altar of success.

The more time we spent together the more Josh began to trust me and appreciate the perspective of an older, more experienced person. Soon, what had begun as a pastoral relationship, evolved into a full-blown mentoring relationship.

In addition to his marriage problems, Josh felt caught between two cultures: his father's British culture (which included many years at boarding school) and his mother's American culture. As someone who has lived in both countries myself, I understood the difficulties associated with a trans-Atlantic lifestyle. Josh never really fit in with his British contemporaries, even though he had been schooled in England. While he liked the U.S. (and married an American girl while at Harvard) and saw much of his mother's family (especially during the holidays) he didn't feel American either. All of this was further complicated by the fact that his parents travelled constantly and were simply never around (although their presence was keenly felt, especially when the subject of career choices came up for discussion). In the end, I became a kind of father-figure to Josh, which is perhaps the most challenging role a mentor can play, especially when a mentoree's parents are still alive. While it is an honor to be trusted and respected by someone such as Josh it's important for a mentor to respect the exceptional nature of a parent-child relationship and never come between (or even be seen to come between) a parent and their child (even an adult child).

What lay at the heart of my mentoring relationship with Josh however, was his fascination with my history of simultaneously balancing a career in business with a career in the academy and the responsibilities of being an ordained pastor. Josh had many varied interests himself and while he was quite sure that a career in the academy wasn't in his future, he wasn't sure what he wanted to do after he left Oxford. He was intrigued by the business world and often asked me probing questions about how companies work, how decisions are made and why companies succeed or fail. But he was also keenly interested in the plight of the poor and wanted to explore ways in which enterprise might be used as a vehicle for the alleviation of poverty and the promotion of human flourishing.

Josh's mind was always at work and full of ideas, but he was incredibly disorganized and as I saw a bit of myself at that age in Josh, I knew from experience that he would have to develop excellent time management skills if he was going to pursue a multi-faceted life-style. In my experience as a chaplain, I have found that many students are quite poor at planning their days and Josh was no exception. However, instead of focusing on tactical issues (i.e. specific tasks), I chose instead to work on strategic issues (i.e. priorities). I encouraged Josh to consider what was genuinely important in the long run and to schedule his activities according to those long-term priorities. That meant putting godly pursuits first; (important) relationships next; his research next and his other interests last. As simple and logical as that may seem, it is not an easy message to communicate to someone who is both brilliant and impulsive. However, this is an area where Josh and I definitely made progress over the years.

Next, I was able to mentor Josh in his role as a leader within his community of Christian peers. While he didn't regularly attend church, Josh was still a committed Christian and was respected by others for his biblical fluency and knowledge of theological issues. However, he wasn't terribly adept at developing close personal relationships; so I set about re-enforcing his responsibility as a Christian to 'love one's neighbor as one's self' and to work toward the building of Christian community within the academy. To that end I encouraged Josh to accept a position as a Junior Dean at one of the theological colleges where he would be required to lead by example and to work with the leadership team of the Oxford Evangelical Pastorate.

Lastly, to satisfy his curiosity about business and to help him explore the benefits of wealth creation as a vehicle for the alleviation of poverty, I encouraged Josh to pursue the area of social entrepreneurship and I continue to work with him on various projects that have both economic and societal benefits, even though he has long since left the University.

This is just one composite example of mentoring relationships that has had positive results. However, there are many other similar relationships at different stages of development. These things take time and one of the challenges of working in a university setting is the transient nature of the community one serves (especially when working with post-graduates whose time at university ranges from one term to three or four years, with most staying only a year or two). However, relationships can develop in that amount of time and thanks to the Internet, they can continue even after the students have left university. I have several mentorees with whom I stay in regular contact and whom I continue to mentor. Which brings me to a very important point about mentoring ministry: it is a long-term commitment, not a temporary assignment. If entered into with faithfulness and love however, mentoring relationships can be an extremely rewarding form of ministry to Generation Y.

8

Faith, Hope, and Love

Writing this book has given me the opportunity to reflect upon the spiritual needs of Generation Y and on my own experience in trying to meet those needs. It has reminded me that young people today are, by and large spiritually bereft. Postmodernism, New Atheism, biblical skepticism and a host of other cultural influences have left them without a meta-narrative upon which to build a life of faith, hope, and love. Instead they have settled for the 'happy midi-narrative' (discussed in a previous chapter) that is unsatisfactory in life and insufficient after death. In short, young people today need the Gospel of Jesus Christ in exactly the same way as every previous and every successive generation—urgently.

My research into this area and my own experience as a university chaplain have taught me that perhaps above all else, any ministry to Generation Y must be a ministry of presence—that is to say, it must reflect the grace of Christ in our own lives and it must be totally authentic. It should also be a ministry that is intellectually as well as spiritually stimulating. It should be a ministry where pastoral care is paramount; where young adults feel comfortable exploring life's most difficult questions together; it should be welcoming and nurturing; it should be a place where the Spirit of God is present and at work in people's lives; and it should be a community of believers and seekers alike.

I also believe that it should be built upon good theology and sound biblical principles but it need not be exclusively Reformed or evangelical. In fact, I would even suggest that it is possible for such a ministry to be both, ecumenical and evangelical, catholic, and Reformed at the same time. It may be ecumenical in its ethos of openness and dialogue while still being under-girded by a foundational belief in the efficacy of the Bible. It may be catholic in its respect for the long-standing traditions of the church while still being inspired by the genius of Reformed thinking and covenant theology.

People sometimes ask how the Church should respond to the arguments against religious belief put forth by the likes of Richard Dawkins, Bart Ehrman, and others. While I hope this question is answered in considerable detail in this book, I believe that the short answer should be 'head-on'. Christians have nothing to fear from the enemies of Christianity regardless of their credentials. However, defenders of the faith must 'put on the full armor of God' (Ephesians 6:11-13) and be ready to do battle in the marketplace of ideas. As such, I believe that part of any ministry to Generation Y should include a boot camp of sorts for those seeking to hone their apologetic skills (1 Peter 3:15) as well as a place for nurture and support in an ever-hostile environment. At the Oxford American Mission, we used our weekly apologetics group for that purpose, but there are many organizations that do an excellent job in this area, such as the Gotham Fellowship program at Redeemer Presbyterian Church and the Centre for Christian Apologetics, a joint venture between the Ravi Zacharias Trust and Wycliffe Hall, Oxford, to name but two. These organizations offer a wide range of training courses (some that come with an accreditation) for church leaders from around the world who want to make apologetics a central part of their Christian witness. What they offer is absolutely invaluable to those seeking to reach Generation Y with the Gospel.

I also believe that ministries of this sort need not (and perhaps should not) be done in isolation. One of my greatest concerns for the Church today is the branding of different ministries. We may be operating in a marketplace of ideas but we shouldn't act as though we are competing in a market for souls with other churches and Christian organizations. My experience in Oxford has convinced me that ministry to Generation Y is best done in *partnership* with other like-minded ministries, including local churches, seminaries, theological colleges and national and/or international organizations. The Oxford American Mission would have never gotten off the ground were it not for the cooperation, support and partnership of the Oxford University Graduate Christian Union, the Oxford Evangelical Pastorate; local churches (such as St. Aldates, St. Ebbes, St. Andrews and St. Clements) and their pastors; the Trinity Forum and the Veritas Forum; as well as the aforementioned Zacharias Trust, OICCU, the Oxford Centre for Mission Studies, Friends International, and others. There is strength in numbers and one of the most effective and satisfying things about my work in Oxford was the cooperation and collegiality of everyone involved.

If the Church today is going to be successful in reaching the next generation of leaders; and be obedient to Jesus' command to 'make disciples' (especially among Generation Y), I believe the key to that success will be found in three things: faith, hope, and love: faith, first and foremost in God, Father, Son, and Holy Spirit and in the power and efficacy of his holy and inspired Word. I believe we should have faith too, in Christianity's truth claims, our creeds and confessions; our traditions; and our institutions, especially the local church.

I also think we should have hope, not only in the results of our efforts but hope in Generation Y itself. My experience of dealing with the people of this generation is that they are extremely bright, engaged, well educated, sensitive, open-minded, and desperately in search of meaning and purpose in their lives. The more time I spend with them, the more optimistic I am about the future, especially when I see them live their lives for Christ and use their energy and skills for kingdom purposes.

Lastly, everything we do must be thoroughly rooted in and motivated by love, which as the Apostle Paul reminds us will be evidenced by an abundance of patience, kindness, grace, goodness, honesty and above all, selflessness. That's what love is all about and in my opinion, that kind of Christian witness is irresistible; not only to Generation Y, but to everyone who experiences it.

Bibliography

Allender, Dan. *Leading With a Limp*. Colorado Springs. Waterbrook Press. 2006.

Barnes, Kenneth J. *The Deployment of Dual Career Ministers as Corporate Chaplains in a Post-industrial Society*. MPhil Thesis. University of London. 2002.

Bledsoe, A.T. *A Theodicy; or Vindication of the Divine Glory*. New York. Nelson and Phillips. 1853.

Blocher, Henri. *Evil and the Cross*. Downers Grove. Intervarsity. 1990.

Brenton, Robert. 'The Apologetic Programme of Cornelius Van Til as an Assault Against the Apologetic Tradition' *Apologia*, 5.2 (1996), pp. 25–30.

Bridger, Francis. *Why Can't I have Faith: working out dis-belief in the postmodern world*. London, Triangle. 1998.

Calvin, John. *Institutes of the Christian Religion*. Grand Rapids. Eerdmans. 1983.

Chung, D. and N. de Mel, *An Outline for the Adoption of a Council of Advisors to the Graduate Christian Union*. Unpublished. 2005.

Collins-Mayo, Sylvia, et al. *The Faith of Generation Y*. London. Church House Publishing. 2010.

Covey, Stephen R. *Principle-Centered Leadership*. New York. Fireside. 1990.

Dawkins, Richard. *The Selfish Gene*. Oxford. Oxford University Press. 2006.

Demarest, Bruce. *Soul Guide: following Jesus as spiritual director*. Colorado Springs. NavPress. 2003.

Dictionary of Scottish Church History and Theology. Downers Grove. Intervarsity. 1993.

Ehrman, Bart. *God's Problem: How the Bible Fails to Answer Our Most Important Question – Why We Suffer*. New York. HarperCollins. 2008 Kindle Edition.

Ehrman, Bart. *Misquoting Jesus*. New York. HarperCollins. 2009 Kindle Edition.

Feinberg, J.S. *The Many Faces of Evil*. Grand Rapids. Zondervan. 1979.

Flanagan, K. and P. Jupp. *Postmodernity, Sociology and Religion*. London. MacMillan Press. 1996.

Greenslade, S.L. *Shepherding the Flock*. London. SCM. 1967.

Bibliography

Gupta, Sunil Unny. *Mentoring, a practitioner's guide to touching lives*. New Delhi. Sage. 2006.

Heifetz, R. and M. Linsky. *Leadership On the Line: staying alive through the dangers of leading*. Boston. Harvard Business School Press. 2002 Kindle edition.

Horsfall, Tony. *Mentoring for Spiritual Growth*. Abingdon. Bible Reading Fellowship. 2008.

John Paul II. *Crossing the Threshold of Hope*. New York. Alfred A. Knopf. 1994.

Kerry, T. and S. Mayes. *Issues in Mentoring*. London. Routledge. 1995.

Kline, Meredith. *Kingdom Prologue*. Two Age Press. 2000 Web Edition.

Lucas, Sean. 2011. *Grace-Centered Leadership*. Reformed Theological Seminary Lectures. Jackson, MS. Delivered January 10–14,·2011.

Mallison, John. *Mentoring to Develop Disciples and Leaders*. Milton Keynes. Scripture Union. 1998.

Marshall, David. *The Truth Behind the New Atheism*. Eugene. Harvest House Publishers. 2007.

McGrath, Alister. *Bridge Building: Effective Christian Apologetics*. Leicester. Intervarsity Press. 1992.

———. *The Twilight of Atheism: the rise and fall of disbelief in the modern world*. New York. Doubleday. 2004.

———. *The Dawkins Delusion?* London. SPCK. 2007.

Metaxas, Eric. *Bonhoeffer: Pastor, Martyr, Prophet, Spy*. Nashville. Thomas Nelson. 2010 Kindle edition.

Moore, Charles E. (ed.). *Provocations: spiritual writings of Kierkegaard*. Farmington. Plough Publishing. 2007.

Oden, Thomas. *Pastoral Theology*. New York. HarperCollins. 1982.

Reventlow, H.G. and Y. Hoffman. *The Problem of Evil and its Symbols in Jewish and Christian Tradition*. London. T&T Clark International. 2004.

Savage, Sara et al. *Making Sense of Generation Y*. London. Church House Publishing. 2006.

Sire, James W. *Habits of the Mind*. Dower's Grove. Intervarsity Press. 2000.

Van Til, Cornelius. *The Intellectual Challenge of the Gospel*. London. Tyndale. 1950.

Yaconelli, Mark. *Contemplative Youth Ministry*. London. SPCK. 2006.